SECRET PROVIDENCE AND NEWPORT

SECRET PROVIDENCE AND NEWPORT

The Unique Guidebook
to
Providence and Newport's
Hidden Sites, Sounds, & Tastes

Barbara Radcliffe Rogers
Juliette Rogers

WITH PHOTOGRAPHS BY
Linda Rutenberg

ECW PRESS

The publication of *Secret Providence and Newport* has been generously supported by the Canada Council, the Ontario Arts Council, and the Government of Canada through the Book Publishing Industry Development Program. **Canadä**

© ECW PRESS, 2002.

All rights reserved. No part of this publication may be reproduced, stored in a retrieval system, or transmitted in any form by any process — electronic, mechanical, photocopying, recording, or otherwise — without the prior written permission ECW PRESS.

NATIONAL LIBRARY OF CANADA CATALOGUING IN PUBLICATION DATA

Rogers, Barbara Radcliffe

Secret Providence & Newport: the unique guidebook to Providence & Newport's hidden sites, sounds, & tastes

Includes index.

ISBN 1-55022-490-5

1. Providence (R.I.) — Guidebooks. 2. Newport (R.I.) — Guidebooks.
I. Rogers, Juliette. II. Title. III. Title: Secret Providence and Newport.
F89.P93R63 2002   917.45'20444   C2001-903592-6

Original series design: Paul Davies, ECW Type and Art, Oakville, Ontario.
Copyediting: Laura Byrne Paquet.
Typesetting: Martel *en-tête*.
Imaging and cover: Guylaine Régimbald – SOLO DESIGN.
Printed by Transcontinental.

Distributed in Canada by General Distribution Services, 325 Humber College Boulevard, Etobicoke, Ontario M9W 7C3.

Distributed in the United States by Independent Publishers Group, 814 North Franklin Street, Chicago, Illinois, 60610.

Published by ECW PRESS
2120 Queen Street East, Suite 200, Toronto, Ontario M4E 1E2.

ecwpress.com

PRINTED AND BOUND IN CANADA

TABLE OF CONTENTS

Secret Providence: Introduction 11
Secret Newport: Introduction 14
How this book is organized 16

Secret Providence

SECRET...

AEROBICS 21
ANTIQUES 21
ART 23
ATTIC 24
B&B 25
BAPTIST 25
BASTILLE DAY 27
BEACHCOMBING 27
BLACK HERITAGE 28
BONFIRES 28
BOOKWORM 29
BRUNCH 29
CAROUSELS 30
CASUAL 31
CDs 32
CHICKEN 32
CHINESE 33
CHINESE JAZZ VENUE 34
CHRISTMAS 34
CINEMA 35
CISIL 36
CLAY 36
COFFEE SHOP 37
COP CLOWN 39
CORN ROWS 40
CRUISES 40
CURIOSITIES 42
DEN OF SPOOKINESS 42
DOME 43
DOUGHBOYS 44

EDGAR ALLEN POE 44	ITALIAN 64
ETHNIC 45	JUNGLE 65
FACADES 46	KINK 66
FAMILY TREE 47	LABOR DAY 67
FINGERNAIL ART 47	LEAF PEEPING 68
FISH & CHIPS 48	LEGS AND EGGS 68
FLOATING B&B 48	LIFE EXPECTANCY CLOCK 69
FOLK 48	LLAMAS 69
FONDUE 49	LORT 70
FRANCO-AMERICAN 50	MANDOO 71
FREE MUSIC 50	MANSIONS 72
GALLERIES 51	MARINARA 74
GAME GEEKS 52	MOLLUSKS 75
GARDENS 52	MONASTERY 75
GAY AND LESBIAN 55	NECESSITIES 76
GIFTS 56	NIGHT LIFE 76
GREENS 56	PADDLES 77
GUIDES 57	PAGAN BIKE RENTALS 80
HIGH CHURCH 57	PAGODA 81
HIPPOS 58	PAPAYA 82
HOLY HOSTELRY 58	PARK 83
HORSES 59	PARKING 83
HOUSES 59	PARROTS 84
H.P. LOVECRAFT 61	PASTA 86
ICE 63	PAWSOX 86
ICE CREAM 63	PORTUGUESE 87

PRANKS 88	SUKIYAKI 105
PUBLIC BUILDINGS 90	SWEET TOOTH 105
RARE BOOKS 90	SWORDS AND SOLDIERS 107
RECIPES 92	
REP 93	TEA PARTIES 108
REVOLUTION 93	THAI 108
RHODE ISLANDIANA 94	THEATERS RESTORED 109
RIVERBOAT 95	TIME TO STAY AWAY 111
SAAG 95	TRAILS 111
SAFARI 96	TRANSPORT 112
SEWING AND KNITTING 98	TREASURE TROVES 112
	VEGETARIAN 113
SHEETS 99	VENICE 115
SHOPPING 99	VICTORIAN 115
SMOKE-FREE GREASY SPOON 100	VIEWS 117
	VINEYARDS 118
SMOKING SECTION 100	WEDDING RECEPTIONS 118
SNAILS 101	WEEKNIGHT DEAL 119
SOUP 102	WIENERS 119
STROLL 103	WILDFLOWERS 121
SUBTERRANEAN DUCKPINS 103	WINTER LIFT 121
	WISE WOMEN 122

Secret Newport

SECRET...

ABLUTIONS 125
ACCESS 125
AERIE 126
AL FRESCO 127
AMBROSIA 128
AMERICA'S CUP 128
ANCESTORS 129
ANIMALS 131
ANIME 132
AROMAS 133
ART 133
ARTILLERY 134
ARTIST 134
ASTRAL BODIES 136
AWFUL-AWFUL 138
B&B 138
BACKSTAIRS 139
BASEBALL 141
BEACHES 141
BIRDS 143
BOOKSTORES 144
BREAD PUDDING 145

BREAKFASTS 145
CAMPING 147
CEILINGS 147
CHAPELS 148
CHASM 149
CHEAP LUNCH 150
CHIC 151
CHOWDAH 151
CHURCHES 153
CLIFF WALK 154
COACHES 155
COFFEE 155
COLONIAL 156
CRAB CAKES 158
CROWD CONTROL 158
DEALS 159
FINDS 160
FISH 161
FISH & CHIPS 162
FOLK ART 162
'40S 163
FORTS 164

FREE MANSIONS 165	NECESSITIES 195
FRIED CLAMS 167	NEW AMERICAN 196
FUSION 167	OASIS 196
GARDENS 168	OYSTERS 197
GLASS 171	PACK RATS 197
GRAVES 171	PADDLES 198
GREEK 173	PASSAGE 199
HISTORY 173	PETS 199
HOOCH 175	PHOTOGRAPHY 200
IRISH 176	PICNICS 201
ITALIAN 177	PIZZA 203
JAPANESE 178	PLANTS 203
JAZZ 179	PLAYGROUNDS 204
JEWELRY 180	PLAYHOUSE 205
JONNYCAKES 181	POLO 205
JUDAICA 181	ROOFTOPS 206
KIDS' STUFF 183	ROYALTY 207
KITCHEN 185	SAILING 208
KITES 186	SAILORS 210
LOBSTERS 186	SALVATION 210
MANSIONS 187	SCRIMSHAW 211
MILL 189	SEAFOOD 212
MONKEYS 190	SEATS 213
MOVIES 191	SLAVES 213
MURDERS 192	SNOBS 214
MUSEUMS 193	SOCKS 215

STATUARY 216	TREASURE 224
STYLE 217	TREES 225
SURF 218	VEAL 226
SURPLUS 218	VILLAGE 227
SWEETS 219	VINTAGE BOATS 227
TEA 219	VIVE LA FRANCE 228
TENNIS 220	WHEELS 229
TIKI BAR 222	WINDMILL 230
TOURS 222	YACHTS 231
TRANSPORT 223	

Secret Future 232
Photo Sites 233
Subject Index 234
Alphabetical Index 243

SECRET PROVIDENCE AND NEWPORT

What do these two cities have in common? They were both founded before the United States began. They're both on the water. They're both in Rhode Island. And, however hard we try, the list stops there.

This total difference between its two subjects has made this book doubly fun to research and write. We use the word "research" very loosely. Neither of us can tell you exactly when we first noticed the funny little chair on the top of the moon gate of Chateau-sur-Mer, heard the rumor that the Hay Library had a book bound in human skin, or were puzzled by the parrots at Sabin Point. We didn't actually go out looking for a lot of our Newport and Providence secrets. We just knew them.

But a lot of the secrets here were new ones to us. When we started doing this book, and told our friends what we were up to, they began saying things like, "Of course, you wouldn't put this in the book, but . . ." And their secrets were out. We are firm believers in equal opportunity, and think that the secrets of our nearest and dearest have just as much right to be aired as our own.

SECRET PROVIDENCE: INTRODUCTION

Providence hides a lot of secrets. No longer the run-down, washed-up city whose industries have all closed down or moved out, Providence has also not fallen into the temptation to "re-invent" itself. Even back in the 1970s, when other cities were gutting their downtowns in a frenzy of destruction called "urban renewal," and replacing fine old buildings with concrete boxes, Providence didn't. The reasons were more fiscal than aesthetic — the city was on the financial skids from losing so much of its industrial base and couldn't afford the bulldozers and construction projects needed to renew its urbanity.

So the city covered many of the downtown buildings with new storefronts — big, ugly 1970s storefronts — and left the originals hidden underneath. There, a new generation of architecture students from the Rhode Island School of Design found them — like a giant stone, brick, and cast iron textbook waiting to be opened — not five blocks from their campus. So the core of downtown Providence (which we call Downcity) is a glorious array of buildings rich in the architectural details of several styles and periods.

Against this background, Providence began to do really unlikely things, like uncover the river running through it all this time that nobody knew about. It's hard to believe a city can have a secret river, and it's even harder to believe when you see what a swath it and its grassy banks cut through the city center. The roads that used to cover it on a multi-lane bridge have been re-routed, and graceful brick bridges now arch over its waters.

So here we had this new river, these pretty arched bridges, a predominantly Italian population and an off-the-wall mayor (also Italian) looking for a way to liven things up downtown. The result? A gondola. Not a clunky little pseudo-gondola with an electric motor, but a beautiful sleek real one, propelled under the bridges by a single oar in the hands of a skillful gondolier.

At first, it got a lot of giggles and a lot of press. Now it gets a lot of passengers, so many that a second one was shipped from Venice. But how to get people to begin strolling up and down the banks in the evening and to treat Waterplace Park as a community living space? With concerts, at first, then with fire.

WaterFire opened a whole new world — 20 nights a year when people gather to do nothing in particular. There's no "best place" to watch it from, and it changes with every step you take, so the best way to enjoy this spectacle is to wander up and down the riverbanks and over the bridges. From sunset to midnight, it's magic.

WaterFire's very democratic — no reviewing stand, no reserved strip of wall for important people to perch on. Our whole family was strolling the banks one Memorial Day weekend during WaterFire and Julie said, "See those two men coming toward us? The one on the right's the president of the European Union."

So whether by design or accident, Providence didn't "re-invent" itself. Instead, it took a scrub brush to what it already had and capitalized on one thing it had in spades: a lively and indomitable population. Nothing is impossible if you've got the people.

We've come here from all over. Our ancestors may have come from the farms of Quebec to run the mills along the Blackstone, or fled half-starved from the blighted potato fields of Ireland, or escaped from the Holocaust or from guerrillas in the Guatemalan highlands. Or they may have descended from the renegade Bostonians who came with Roger Williams. Or we may be renegade Bostonians ourselves, looking for a smaller, more intimate city to call home where we don't have to give up our bookstore and ice cream habits.

The music, performance, and entertainment scene in Providence is nothing short of exhausting. Whatever your taste, you're likely to find evenings when you must choose between two or three options. To keep abreast of these, the best source is the "Live This Weekend" section of the *Providence Journal*, or the *Providence Phoenix*, the city's alternative paper, which you can pick up free in many places.

For information in advance, or when you first hit town, contact the **Providence Warwick Convention and Visitors Bureau** in the Convention Center (1 West Exchange Street, Providence, RI 02903;

274-1636 or 1-800-233-1636, www.providencecvb.com). Another office, just for the city, is the **Providence Tourism Council** (55 Dorrance Street, Providence, RI 02903; 861-0100 or 1-800-562-9895, www.tourprovidence.com). Get information and a calendar of events north of the city from the **Blackstone Valley Tourism Council** (175 Main Street, Pawtucket, RI 02860; 724-2200 or 1-800-454-2882, www.tourblackstone.com).

SECRET NEWPORT: INTRODUCTION

Secrets? In Newport? How can there be any secrets left in a place that is so well known and heavily visited? Maybe the dirty laundry of the rich and famous, from the Astors to the von Bulows, has been aired ad infinitum, but the natives and sailors still know a thing or two about where to have breakfast, where to get fresh lobster, where to fly a kite, and where to buy designer labels for less. And those who return year after year for getaway weekends know the coziest rooms to curl up in, the restaurants with the best wine lists, and the beach with room to spread their towels.

Even Bellevue Avenue has its secrets, like which mansions you can see without paying admission and ways to avoid the lines at the others. The great mansions themselves have hidden corners, overlooked treasures, and an endless supply of gossip to share.

What makes Newport so enjoyable to visit is that, for all its past ostentation and present well-heeled yachtsmen, it's a pretty down-to-earth place. When you ask a local for advice on where to eat, you'll get his own personal favorite. While Newporters have their secrets, they're pretty generous about sharing them. And we've been using it as our own private hideaway — it's only 35 minutes from Providence — long enough to have plenty of friends there to guide us, and a lot of secrets of our own. If you read closely, you'll learn which rooms we always request — and why.

Newport's history is a long one, beginning well before the Revolution. The city boomed in colonial days, its harbor filled with ships of the China and Triangle trades. It suffered a long and devastating British occupation, when both residents and occupiers burned many of its buildings and all its trees as firewood just to survive the winter.

The first summer visitors were wealthy Charleston merchants who escaped the summer heat in Newport's fresh breezes. Then the literati arrived from Boston, followed by the new American aristocracy, mostly from New York. It was their reign that put Newport on the map forever, because even when they left, their palaces remained. So did the thousands of immigrants and others who had come to Newport to build, decorate, or work at these mansions, and whose cultures give Newport its variety and color today. Newport is a living and very livable little city.

The same attractions Newport always had for visitors are still there: the temperate weather, a good sheltered harbor, beaches, fresh seafood, and ocean views. Newporters — helped by the financial support of the many wealthy people whose families still fill a surprising number of the villas and mansions — have preserved and restored a treasury of buildings representing America's primary architects and decorative styles of the past four centuries. Not one example, but several, exist here by architects from Peter Harrison to Stanford White.

Not only can visitors tour many of these homes to see their original and restored interiors, but they can also sink into bed at night in extraordinary — even museum-quality — Colonial, Victorian, Arts and Crafts, Art Deco, and Gilded Age settings. Or they can retire to an island and sleep in the solitary peace of the keeper's cottage in a lighthouse.

If you are planning a trip to Newport, contact the Newport Convention and Visitors' Bureau (23 America's Cup Avenue, Newport, RI 02840, 849-8048 or 1-800-326-6030, info@GoNewport.com, www.GoNewport.com). The visitors' information center is easy to locate, right on the waterfront on America's Cup Avenue. It should be your first stop, not only to pick up a map, but also to get the latest information on events and to make reservations for any tours and some of the mansions. The small weekly *Newport This Week* contains a calendar of events that includes who is playing at local clubs and pubs.

For information on the mansions managed by the Preservation Society of Newport County (The Breakers, Rosecliff, The Elms, and others), contact their offices (424 Bellevue Avenue, Newport, RI 02840, 847-1000, www.NewportMansions.org).

HOW THIS BOOK IS ORGANIZED

We knew you'd wonder, especially when you started looking for a place to eat lunch, rent a kayak, or get your hair braided. So that's how we've organized the book. Useful, everyday categories like Lort and Corn Rows and Paddles and Chinese Jazz Venue and Kink and Llamas are listed alphabetically, right there where you'd look first when you needed any of those things. Brunch and Marinara and Sheets . . . you know, the kinds of things you'd look up in the Yellow Pages, if only they were listed that way.

HOW THIS BOOK IS ORGANIZED

Because we recognize that what we consider to be the secret — and therefore the heading for that entry — may not be what you're looking for in a hurry, we have also listed things by their more generic categories, such as restaurants, accommodations, and shopping. We have separated these listings by city, since when you're in Providence, it doesn't do you much good to know where the public loos are in Newport. These lists are at the back of the book.

All — or almost all — telephone numbers are in the 401 area code. When they're not, we have added the code. Speaking of details, we haven't included the opening hours of places, except in rare cases. That's not because we're lazy. Usually, we did put them in our notebooks, but hours of opening change faster than New England weather, and we have learned from long, sad experience that having outdated hours in a book is worse than having none. If we don't put them in, you'll call and get them if they're important. If they are in the book, you will trust them and then be really annoyed at us when they are wrong. But if a place habitually has really crazy hours or closes unusually early, we're likely to mention it.

Opening times aren't the only things that change. By their nature, restaurants and shops — especially the small, quirky ones that are most likely to be included in a *Secret Guide* — come and go. Some go faster than others, but even places that have been on the same corner for years will, three days after the publication of one of our books, get an itch to move down the street — or out of town. So don't blame us. These places were here when we wrote about them. Before you go out of your way, it's always a good idea to call. That's why we give you the phone number. If it's been disconnected, consider this a bad sign.

One more thing: if there are two authors, how come the secrets that follow nearly all use the first person singular? It's a simple rule of physics, perhaps not quite as significant as the Pythagorean Theorem, but significant nonetheless. Two hands can't hold the same pencil. To bring that up to date, it's hard for 20 fingers to use the same keyboard at the same time. So each secret was written by one of us. Besides, we think the royal "we" sounds pompous and silly. So this is the last place you'll read it, except when it's used in the context of one of us and our respective Significant Other, hereinafter known as S.O. Some of our little secrets make them blush, and neither of them wishes to be further identified.

SECRET PROVIDENCE

SECRET
AEROBICS
✦

Runners love Providence for its scenic, wide and traffic-free pathways along the river and through **Waterplace Park**. Bridges offer a chance to vary the length of loops, and, for an extra workout, many streets on the east bank head directly up the hill. **Benefit Street** is the city's most historic route, stretching from Wickenden Street to North Main Street, and entirely lined with trees and restored homes.

Runners with an eye for landscape design can admire the artistry of America's best-known designer, Frederick Law Olmsted (of Central Park fame), on the park-like "center strip" of **Blackstone Boulevard**. It's at the far northeast edge of the city, past the Brown University campus. Well-landscaped Victorian and Art Deco homes line both sides of the street and you'll share the strip with a few other runners.

SECRET
ANTIQUES
✦

If you really want to see the best — the finest examples of early American cabinetmakers' works that set the standard to which others are compared — see the furnishings in the **John Brown House** (52 Power Street, at Benefit Street, 331-8575). John Brown was a major player in Providence's profitable China Trade, and his brother was an architect. The brother designed the house and John furnished and

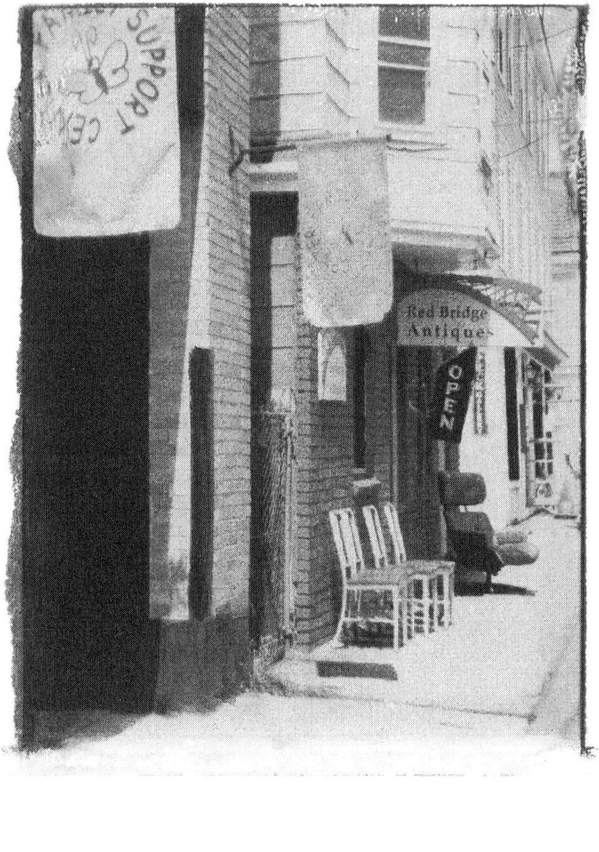
SUPPORT
Red Bridge
Antiques
OPEN

decorated it with the best the colonies could offer and the best he could import.

For those who could afford it, life could be quite gracious and comfortable in colonial Providence, and in this house you get a sense of what that 18th-century life was like.

Another secret here: for free admission, go between 5 and 9 PM on the third Thursday of each month, except December (see information on Gallery Night under "Secret Art").

SECRET ART
❧

Between the colleges — Rhode Island School of Design's campus is smack in the middle of Providence, while Brown University and Providence College crown the hilltops on either side — and the plethora of private galleries that keep local walls smartly decorated, you'll never want for an art fix. Most of it you can see without charge. In fact, you can even get to the art on a free trolley on the third Thursday of each month (except December), and get free parking and wine, too. On **Gallery Night**, three **ArTrolleys** (751-2628) shuttle the art-smart between a dozen art galleries, events, antique shops, and museums. A guide on board describes what's being shown at each stop, so you can make informed choices. Get on or off at any or all stops on the trolleys' continuous circuit until 9 PM. The first run begins at 5 PM, at Freeman Park at Westminster and Mathewson Streets. For more on art galleries, see "Secret Galleries."

Exhibits change often at the **David Winton Bell Gallery** (List Art Building, 64 College Street, 863-2932). Admission to retrospectives, photography shows, and special collections of contemporary and historic art is free.

You probably wouldn't think to look for an art exhibit inside a charming Victorian casino in Slater Park, but it's the home of the **Rhode Island Watercolor Society** (Armistice Boulevard, Pawtucket, 726-1876), and its gallery and learning center. If you step inside, you've a treat in store. Rhode Island and New England watercolorists exhibit here, and the paintings spread over two floors are for sale.

SECRET ATTIC
✤

Doorways on Wickenden Street lead into vast accumulations of antiques, collectibles, nostalgia, and stuff of every vintage — it's like poking around in someone's never-ending attic. They range from fine antiques to stuff so barely old that it brings exclamations of "I used to have one of these" from Brown freshmen. I never fail to add another vintage kitchen utensil to my collection at **This & That Shop** (236 Wickenden Street, 861-1394), a co-op whose seasonally inspired window displays always make me stop. It has mostly small stuff, and a whole room full of kitchen and dishy things. The biggest concentration of stores is at the far end of Wickenden, where it meets Governor Street; one shop there specializes in old lighting fixtures and lamps, a couple in furniture.

SECRET
B & B
❖

Providence does not have the proliferation of in-town B&Bs that some cities do, which makes the **State House Inn** (43 Jewett Street, 785-1235) all the more welcome. In a restored century-old home, rooms are well furnished in Shaker reproductions and American primitive art. Full breakfast includes a hot dish, fresh fruit, and baked goods. It's just behind the State House, in a neighborhood of historic homes.

SECRET
BAPTIST
❖

When a church uses the word "first" in its name, it signifies that it is the first church of that denomination in town. But for Providence's **First Baptist Meeting House** (75 North Main Street, 454-3418), "first" means a great deal more. It is the first Baptist church, period. Both the oldest congregation of the faith and the oldest surviving meeting house, it is the "Mother Church" of Baptists everywhere.

The faith — the Baptist Society — was founded by Roger Williams (who also founded the city and state) in Providence, and the present building rose in 1775. Its 185-foot stepped steeple was built on the ground in only three days, using a telescoping system. The interior of the church is one of America's finest examples of Georgian architec-

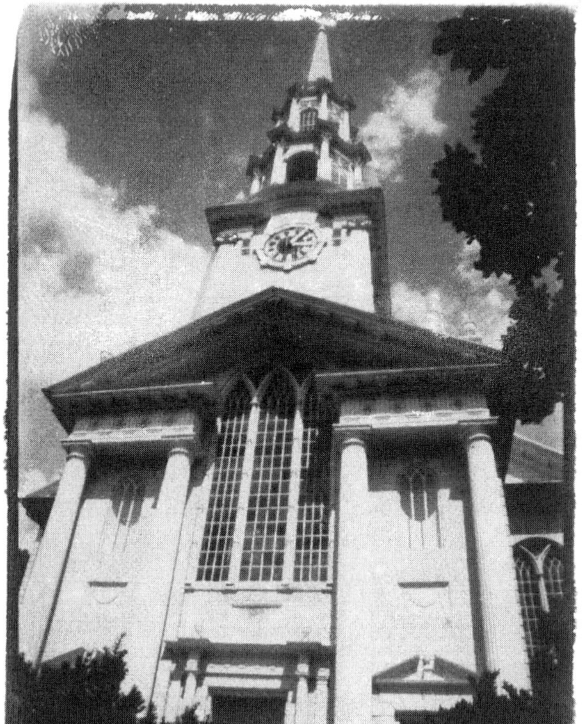

ture. A brochure for a self-guided tour outlines more of the building's history and architecture, and Sunday worship services at 11 AM are followed by a guided tour.

SECRET
BASTILLE DAY
※

Providence celebrates the storming of the Bastille on July 14 with the **Great Bastille Day Restaurant Race** (273-8953). Waiters from the state's restaurants compete in this test of speed, each balancing a tray of filled wine glasses. I always wonder whether they are using fine French vintages for this.

SECRET
BEACHCOMBING
※

Goddard Memorial State Park (Ives Road, off Forge Road, Warwick, 884-2010) follows the coast of Greenwich Cove, overlooking East Greenwich. In addition to trails, shoreline fishing, picnicking, bridle paths, riding rings, and boat ramps, the park has sandy swimming beaches. During a low or receding tide, the shoreline of the cove is a good place for beachcombing. Tides sweep drifting objects along the cove and leave them on the sand.

SECRET
BLACK HERITAGE
✤

The **Rhode Island Black Heritage Society** (202 Washington Street, 751-3490) focuses on the unique role Rhode Island played in early Black American history. Although slave holding was not rare in neighboring northern colonies and states, Rhode Island was the only one with a plantation system, so slaves were far more common. The society's displays and exhibitions illustrate this diverse Black history, while extensive historical archives are available for research. A brochure available here lists important Black history sites in Rhode Island. The **Langston Hughes Center for the Arts and Education** (1 Hilton Street, 598-5422) is a performance venue as well as a teaching center, spotlighting the contribution of African-Americans to all areas of the arts.

SECRET
BONFIRES
✤

Anything that's right there in plain sight, like 97 bonfires burning all at once in the middle of a river in the middle of New England's second-largest city, is pretty hard to keep secret. I just hope word of this doesn't leak out before the book is published, so you'll see it here first. There's a good chance it will, though, because only about 15,000 people were with me the last time I went, and the spectacle is only scheduled for 20 times a year, from March through November. Bonfires are lit for **WaterFire** (272-3111, www.waterfire.org) at sunset and kept burning until midnight. Black-clad stokers move along the river in black boats, tossing logs into the metal bins that stand on poles in the water. Music accompanies the show, but mostly people just stroll along the riverbank, chat with friends, and enjoy a convivial evening.

SECRET BOOKWORM

❦

Wayland Square is a funny little neighborhood, with dowdy ladies' apparel sold next door to retro antiques. Starbucks has invaded, but it's around a corner so it's easy to ignore. Turn your eyes instead to **Myopic Books** (5 South Angell Street, 521-5533), a classic used bookstore in a spacious, bright place you could spend all day in. They serve tea here, in a casual sort of way, but mostly leave you to your own devices, roaming the stacks. The store's strengths seem to lie in the strengths of Providence's student populations — arts and non-fiction are well covered, and that perennial favorite, cookbooks, puts up a good showing.

SECRET BRUNCH

❦

Nothing occupies a sleep-in Sunday morning quite so satisfyingly as a leisurely brunch of Portuguese sweet bread French toast or an omelette rich in imported cheese. At **Rue de l'Espoir** (99 Hope Street, 751-8890), you'll find crepes, waffles, and all the usual breakfast favorites, always with some touch or ingredient that makes them stand out above plain old breakfast dishes. The casual restaurant is also open for lunch and dinner, with both full and bistro menus.

You will have to wait two hours to be seated in **Brickway on Wickenden** (234 Wickenden Street, 751-2477). It is an anti-secret, at least to people who live in the neighborhood. Its neon orange exterior ensures it is never overlooked. But it has yummy things, like a mountain of lox, cukes, tomato, red onion, and cream cheese to go with your bagel, or pancakes with banana, chocolate chips, or blueberries, or huevos rancheros. Service is surprisingly prompt and friendly, which redeems the wait considerably, as it shows the place hasn't developed too high an opinion of itself. Brickway is thronged by students not too hung over to eat on Sunday mornings. Aim early, aim late, or aim to wait.

SECRET CAROUSELS

An immigrant furniture carver named Charles I.D. Looff, who carved 27 goats, zebras, storks, camels, and horses and put them onto a revolving platform at Coney Island in 1875, could never have dreamed how many generations of children (and big kids, too) would delight in his invention. He soon built another of his horse-turned rides at Bullock Point in East Providence, and another at Roger Williams Park in Providence. Within 20 years, Looff had his own 50-acre park at Riverside in East Providence.

In 1910, the Roger Williams carousel was moved to Pawtucket, operating until neglect and disrepair shut it down in 1967. Amid official mutterings about tearing it down, it was saved by public outcry (even outrage) and refurbished. You can ride the **Slater Park Looff Carousel** (Newport Avenue, Pawtucket, 728-0500, ext. 257) on spring and fall weekends and daily during the summer, choosing from 44 horses, three dogs, one camel, one giraffe, and two benches. All but one horse are original Looff figures.

Considered the finest example of these early carousels in existence, the **Crescent Park Carousel** (Bullock Point Avenue, East Providence, off Route 103, 434-3311) is registered as a National Historic Landmark. The chariots, with intertwined serpents, are the finest remaining and were made by Looff's son. This Looff carousel, with all original horses, dates from 1895, when Looff built the park. Each intricately hand carved and hand painted, no two of the 66 figures are alike. The jeweled trappings still gleam, attracting not just children to its inexpensive rides. Like its Slater Park counterpart, the carousel is open on spring and fall weekends and daily through the summer.

SECRET
CASUAL
∻

When you're in the mood for something good to eat, prepared with a little imagination, that won't overtax your palate or your wardrobe, think of **3 Steeple Street** (3 Steeple Street, but enter around the corner on Canal Street, 272-3620). It won't overtax your wallet, either, and is an especially good choice when you want a light meal in the evening. Some dishes are offered in three different sizes, and you can mix and match soups, salads, and appetizers to create a meal without anyone raising an eyebrow. Sandwiches are good here — the menu caught my attention right away with a BLT that added boursin.

SECRET
CDs
❦

Need new music? Or need money for old music? Buy, sell, or trade CDs at **Round Again Records** (278 Wickenden Street, 351-6292), or add to your collection of vinyl. This is a good source toward the end of a semester, when financial realities hit college students and they begin to live off the purchases they made in the heady days when parental support checks were more frequent.

SECRET
CHICKEN
❦

Before I tell you where to get it, I'd better tell you what chicken family style is, because it's a phenomenon peculiar to the Blackstone Valley region just north of the city, and most people from East Providence or Greenwich have never heard of it. Traditionally, it is chicken with vegetables and pasta, all served up in big bowls and platters in the middle of the table, where you just dig into it. In restaurants, it sometimes means all-you-can-eat chicken served with all the fixings. But in most restaurants, you can't get it. **Bocce Club** (226 St. Louis Avenue, Woonsocket, 762-0155) serves it, and in a setting as traditionally Italian family as you could ask for. Its dark wood walls and aura of going-out-for-Sunday-dinner prepare you for what you may see on a Sunday afternoon: multi-generational families gathered happily around a table full of *abondanza*, with little girls in fluffy dresses and little boys anxious to be out of reach of aunts who pinch their cheeks. The food is hearty, nicely prepared, traditional Italian-American. Chicken family style is the Sunday favorite, although the restaurant (really a private club) is open for dinner on other nights as well.

SECRET CHINESE

It may seem an unusual center for Chinese culture, but the **Beneficent Congregational Church** (300 Weybosset Street, 331-9844), the oldest building in Downcity, sat in the heart of a Chinese neighborhood in the late 19th century. Many Chinese joined the congregation, and they maintain a presence today. The church was built in 1808, with the portico and dome added in 1836. If it's open, stop in to see the magnificent chandeliers. The church is the scene of the annual **Chinese New Year Celebration** in February, with folk dances, music, and martial arts.

SECRET
CHINESE JAZZ VENUE
✤

No, the jazz isn't Chinese, but the carved red lacquer and mahogany walls — and the menu of 100-plus favorite and more esoteric entrées — at **Chan's** (267 Main Street, Woonsocket, 765-1900, 762-1364) certainly are. So is the Chan family, who has owned this restaurant for more than a century. If the connection between Chinese food and jazz is puzzling, add the fact that the restaurant sits squarely in the center of a blue-collar, Franco-American mill town. Yet jazz, folk, and blues lovers flock there from Providence, Boston, and beyond to hear the likes of Livingston Taylor, Rose Weaver, Tom Rush, and the New Black Eagles Jazz Band. Each weekend brings at least one live performance, usually on Friday. Call for the schedule, then make a reservation, since space is limited.

SECRET
CHRISTMAS
✤

With the overwhelming abundance of fairs, parties, concerts, festivals, celebrations, and sales that accompanies the holidays, it's a wonder we don't all sleep right through Christmas Day from pure exhaustion. But a couple of events almost get lost in the glitter and blinking lights. The **Annual International Holiday Sale** (8 Stimson Street, 421-7181), usually held the first Saturday in December, brings foods and crafts from all over the world to International House of RI. It's my favorite place to kick off my Christmas shopping with some interesting things I know I won't see elsewhere — and it gives me a chance to stock up on some unique goodies.

And somewhere in the fine print of December calendars you'll find, on the first Monday of the month, the wonderfully inspiring **Latin Christmas Carol Celebration** (863-2123), where you'll hear carols in Latin, classical readings, and instrumental and a capella music. Most recently, it's been held in the First Baptist Meeting House (see "Secret Baptist"), about as perfect a setting as you could find for such lovely music. The concert is free, a gift to the community from Brown University's Department of Classics. Blessed be such Ivy League arcanity.

There's nothing wrong with tinsel — especially when you can get it at a discount. One of Woonsocket's many factory stores, **Tinsel Town and Patioland** (93 Hazel Street, off School Street from Route 126, Woonsocket, 766-5700), is an outlet for makers of holiday decorations (and, in other seasons, for patio and summer furniture manufacturers). Look there for wreaths, garlands, and other trappings of the season to be jolly.

SECRET CINEMA

For the comfort of your favorite squishy armchair or couch, with a full-sized screen and first-run art-house and foreign films, head to the **Cable Car Cinema** (204 South Main Street, 272-3970). Doubling as a cafe with quite respectable pastries and coffee, it sometimes has live performances before movie showings, done by artists who work for tips, like buskers. One time we visited, the performer was a folk-tune guy who looked like he might be in middle management by day. We thought he was upbeat and entertaining, despite the fact that we didn't care for the type of music he played. The surreality and surprise of it was very cool, and we talked more about that than about the movie on the walk home. The Cable Car also hosts film festivals with random themes from time to time.

SECRET CISIL
❦

Kaplan's Bakery (756 Hope Street, 621-8107) is charmingly timeless, as many nooks of Providence can be. Bakers for the city's Jewish community, which is centered on this neighborhood, they make a mean pumpernickel bread, and multiple types of rye, in enormous loaves that you can buy by the half or quarter loaf. Look for the cisil rye, which has caraway seeds. The pastries aren't bad either — the funny, no-nonsense woman who is always behind the counter tells me their éclairs are their best-selling sweet, and they have seasonal specialties too.

SECRET CLAY
❦

Not the clay you make pots from, but the kind you play tennis on: the **Todd Marsilli Tennis Center** (Roger Williams Park, 785-9450) has the state's only public clay courts. They're open daily in the summer and court fees are very reasonable — especially for clay. **Tennis Rhode Island** (70 Boyd Avenue, East Providence, 434-5550, or 636 Centerville Road, Warwick, 828-4450) has indoor courts for nonpurists, open daily from September to Memorial Day.

SECRET
COFFEE SHOP

I considered calling this "Secret Coffee Roasted on the Premises with Baked Goodies Better than Mom's," but it wouldn't fit on one line. **Coffee Exchange** (207 Wickenden Street, 273-1198 or 1-800-632-2339, www.coffeeexchange.com) isn't a big secret, but there is a lot going on under this roof that's less famous than the coffee.

It's a good place to spend your afternoon deciphering 19th-century anthropologists (if it could be said such a place exists at all). No one will bother you, you will not feel guilty for taking up a table, and the music is usually jazz, world music, or classical that won't wreck your concentration. It has been a good place for men to meet men, and women to meet women, although its star may be on the decline on that front. It's *the* place to look for a roommate, either by posting your need for one or cruising the postings to find someone whose quirks mesh with yours. I found a great apartment thanks to these walls. There's a nice outdoor deck, good for people watching when you should be reading your Taylor and Durkheim.

The coffee is Equal Exchange, ensuring that the people who grew the coffee actually got paid for their efforts (there is lots of information

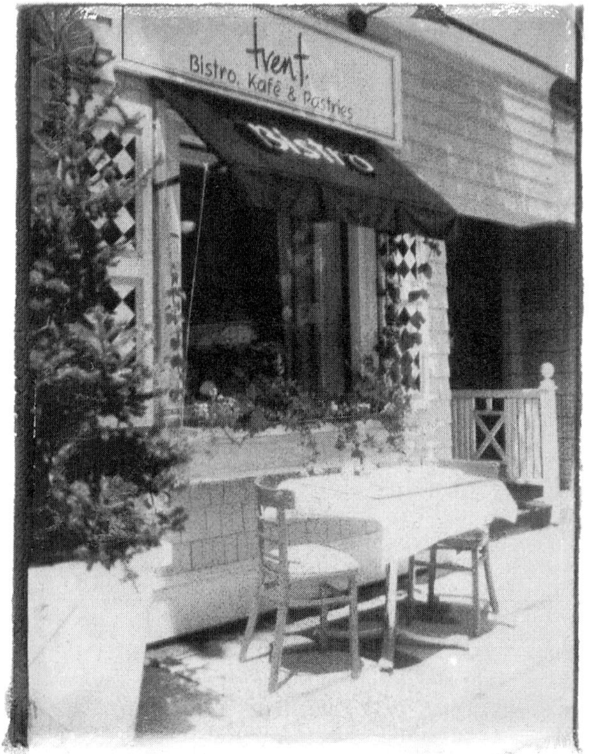
trent
Bistro, Kafé & Pastries
bistro

on that in the cafe). They roast the coffee beans in the back of the cafe; you can peek at the roasting operation when you go to use the restroom (it's in the back room — just walk between the counter and the coffee bins, ahead to the left).

The most astonishing aspect of the place is the baked goods. If I called them pastries, you might assume I meant fussy tarts and pieces of torte, so baked goods it is. They have pound cake, carrot cake, biscotti, cookies, and several very large cookie bars to choose from, and coffee cake and gingerbread, upon occasion. It's all homey stuff, buttery or crispy, and always fresh. The line can be long, the service espresso fuelled, but it's worth it. Nothing like marble pound cake to bribe yourself to get some work done, that's what I say.

SECRET COP CLOWN

One of the bizarre wonders of Providence is that there is a working traffic cop who is also a clown. No foam noses for this gentleman, though — only his honorable uniform and those bright-white gloves like Mickey Mouse and traffic directors wear. The best chance you have of catching his antics is to go to the Columbus Day parade on Federal Hill, where he will be marching as sure as Christopher Columbus was an Italian. His clowning is very physical — a pantomime of traffic direction with silly, skillful tumbles.

Kids adore him, grown-ups scramble for a better view, and I just love to watch this guy who loves to entertain his city so much. The parade is worth seeing for other things too — baton-twirling academies bust their moves, and folkloric dancers from the Dominican Republic and

Bolivia dazzle with brilliant costumes, while music rattles from the pickup truck that carries their banners. Fire trucks glimmer as they pass, and the Budweiser Clydesdales usually come too. You can be guaranteed a sighting of Mayor Buddy Cianci and his toupee.

SECRET
CORN ROWS

We mean the kind in your hair, not the kind they make mazes out of. To have your hair expertly braided — even in stripes, if you're ready for a change of color — go to **Hairspray** (259 Wickenden Street, 273-9210) and ask for an appointment with Lana. Michelle is our pick there for nicely manicured and smartly polished nails.

SECRET
CRUISES

Not content with providing statewide bus service at rock-bottom prices, the Rhode Island Public Transit Authority (RIPTA) now also runs the **water ferry** *Anna* (781-9400, www.ripta.com), which shuttles passengers between Point Street Landing and Newport's Perrotti Park. RIPTA ground transport meets arrivals at each end. Service runs from mid-April through mid-October and the price is under $5. With five departures a day, you can spend a few hours in Newport, stay over, or just enjoy the cheapest scenic cruise in town.

CRUISES

Or travel up the Seekonk River to Pawtucket's Town Landing aboard a pair of riverboat ferries operated by **Water Cruises of Rhode Island** (1-800-619-2628, www.watercruises.com). Point Street Landing is the Providence embarkation point, and the fare for the 45-minute ride (at press time) is an unbelievable two bucks.

SECRET
CURIOSITIES

What I like best about the **Museum of Natural History** (Roger Williams Park, 785-9457) is the room that preserves the wonderfully romantic Victorian gentleman's "cabinet of curiosities" that formed the basis of so many fine museums. This exhibit doesn't just replicate a portion of one; it looks at the world of the Victorian collector. The museum has other permanent exhibits, all nicely done and some interactive, as well as the Cormack Planetarium, which has changing shows.

SECRET
DEN OF SPOOKINESS

Whether you're mopey, perky, ethereal, or industrial goth, slink down the stairs to the underground (I mean that literally) BEDLAM! (183 Angell Street, 351-4731) whenever the neighborhood's collegiate ponytail and white hat crowd gets you down. Matthew, the owner, will likely be behind the counter dispensing fashion tips and clubbing options to a friend — or to you, if you ask. He carries a good selection of new goth threads for many tastes — including punk, if buying ready-made punk clothes isn't antithetical to the whole DIY notion. The back of the store has a carefully selected vintage array, which branches out from black velvet and scarlet lace to include some clothes with wider appeal — you might luck out if rockabilly, neo-swing, or neo-seventies is your scene. I especially commend his choices in men's clothes — while most goth clothiers are 90 percent women's clothes, BEDLAM! is about half and half, giving men a yummy vista of satin and puffy shirts, chain-decked pants, and Victorian coats to choose from. You can order exotic Doc Martens here, though the store regularly stocks only some basics. The location itself seems like a bit of a secret: at the corner of Thayer, look for a sandwich board on the sidewalk directing you to the alley behind Tealuxe, where you will find the stairs.

SECRET DOME

What's so secret about the **State House** (277-2357)? It's pretty hard to hide, with that big dome sticking out above town. And that's the secret — the dome. Ask anybody and you'll get a different answer to the question, "Just how *does* the dome rank in world domedom?" Ask — or look for mentions of it anywhere — and you will learn that it is the second-, third-, or fourth-largest unsupported dome in the world. Which? The only agreement you'll get is that it's not the largest: that title goes to St. Peter's in Rome. Other domes, including those at the Taj Mahal and the Minnesota State Capitol, are sometimes mentioned. Rankings aside, the building is interesting to visit, with a full-length portrait of George Washington by Gilbert Stuart and other historic and artistic miscellany. The library has a carved and gold-leaf ceiling, the House of Representatives chamber is hung with needlepoint tapestries, and in the foyer is a cannon that still has a cannonball inside it, having misfired at the Battle of Gettysburg. The State House is open weekdays, and if you call first you can usually get a guided tour.

SECRET DOUGHBOYS

❖

Maybe it's not a secret if you live here, but how would a stranger in town find this? By following the crowds to Oakland Beach on a hot day, maybe. **Iggy's Doughboys** (737-9459) sits right at the beach, serving up deep-fried blobs of dough that people stand in line for. Clamcakes are the second most popular item on the short menu.

SECRET EDGAR ALLEN POE

❖

A Providence widow, Sarah Whitman, so admired the works of Edgar Allen Poe that she wrote a poem to him, which was published. Poe wrote to her and they corresponded for some time before he came to Providence to lecture at the Franklin Lyceum. Poe fell in love with Mrs. Whitman and courted her in the garden of her home (still standing at 88 Benefit Street) and in the alcoves of the **Providence Athenaeum** (251 Benefit Street, 421-6970), one of America's oldest libraries. It's easy to picture these flirtatious goings-on among the tall shelves and in the recessed galleries.

Although Poe proposed marriage and she accepted, Mrs. Whitman added the condition that he stop drinking. He did not, and she broke the engagement. Poe left Providence brokenhearted but not before writing his poem, "To Helen," which was really to Sarah Whitman. You can visit the Athenaeum and read there Monday through Saturday, although only members can borrow books. You'll find its collections refreshingly unstuffy for so venerable an institution: along with medieval manuscripts from the 1300s and an original set of Audubon's *Birds of America*, the library lists an outstanding collection of erotica.

SECRET ETHNIC

Whatever your own roots, you're likely to find someone who shares them at the **Heritage Day Festival** (277-2669) in September. Groups representing about 30 different ethnicities gather on the State House lawn, where they entertain each other and festival-goers with song, dance, craft demonstrations, and food. The cultural influences that have shaped the city and state may surprise you, and the list continues to grow as each new immigrant group arrives.

SECRET
FACADES
✤

People hardly ever look up as they walk along a city street. Of course, raising your gaze does incur the risk of bumping into people or stepping off a curbstone in front of a bus. But if you don't look up in Downcity, you'll miss some delicious little architectural secrets.

Begin at the **Providence Performing Arts Center** (220 Weybosset Street, 421-2787), which was once the Loews State Theater. Its Beaux Arts facade is well dressed in brick and terra-cotta (and the interior is as resplendently attired in Rococo sculpture). In the center of the street — and you don't have to look up for this one — is the ornate Weybosset Information Center, built in 1914 as public restrooms.

Down the rest of Weybosset, look up to see late 19th-century architectural styles and doodads. Just past The Arcade (see "Secret Shopping"), on your left, is a High Victorian–style facade. Across the street, a former bank is a rare example of an Italian palazzo-style business block, later changed to add storefronts on the first floor. Next to it is the Wilcox Building, which was one of the costliest Providence buildings of its day when it was built, in 1875. The facade and columns are carved in animal and plant themes. At the corner, with the Wilcox Building wrapped around it (another section of it is around the corner, facing onto Wilcox Street), is a Victorian Gothic cast-iron facade. You can't help but look up to notice the disembodied turbaned head above the door of the Turk's Head Building, on the opposite side of the street, looking across toward the Customs House.

SECRET
FAMILY TREE
✤

If your family tree has any Rhode Island branches, you will probably be able to trace them at the **Rhode Island Historical Society Library** (121 Hope Street, 331-8575). Its library of genealogies, histories, newspapers, and documents is one of New England's largest. The society also exhibits artifacts, photos, paintings, and other collections, shown free. There is no charge for use of the research material, either.

SECRET
FINGERNAIL ART
✤

While a lot of Providence beauty shops and salons can make your nails look really classy, if yours are crying out to be adorned in decals, call **Hair-2-E-tan-ity** (1395 Atwood Avenue, Johnston, 943-7373) and ask for Marie Russillo. She's so good that we know a beauty shop way down in Cranston that sends their clients to her for decals. As you might have guessed from the name, you can work on your tan there, too.

SECRET
FISH & CHIPS

As incongruous as Chan's, a couple of blocks away (see "Secret Chinese Jazz Venue"), **Ye Olde English Fish & Chips** (Market Square, Woonsocket, 762-3637) looks very much like its Brit counterparts. The family-owned restaurant serves fish & chips, fish filets, fish cakes, and fish burgers, with chicken for variety. Order your meal and take it to a table. This isn't a place to go for a late supper — it closes around 6:30 PM.

SECRET
FLOATING B&B

The authentic British **Samuel Slater Canal Boat** (724-2200) docks in Valley Falls, just north of Providence, and sleeps four as a cozy B&B. Its red color and low-slung lines are identical to those on the canal boats of England, and the 40-foot vessel is also available for charter cruises. As a B&B, it's open year round.

SECRET
FOLK

Celebrating the many cultures of the immigrants who came to work in the mills of the Blackstone Valley, **Pendragon** (729-1880) is a well-known folk ensemble based at the **Blackstone River Theatre** (1420 Broad Street [Route 114], at Madeira Avenue, Central Falls, 725-9272). Along with Pendragon, the theater is the venue for other New England folk, ethnic, jazz, and blues groups, as well as theater and children's programs. On Friday evenings, there's often a coffee house show in the theater lobby.

SECRET FONDUE

Two Johnson and Wales University–trained chefs met in the kitchen of Al Forno, fell in love, left to open a restaurant together (with the blessing of their old boss), and cooked happily ever after. It could be the plot of the first soap opera in Food Network history, but it's true, and right here in Providence. **Empire** (123 Empire Street, 621-7911) is their place. Its simple, clean, and contemplative decor lets their food be the focus. If you're the sort who likes to make heads turn, order the fondue for two, because it comes on a little cart to hold the pot and dips. The most successful entrees tend to be the meat-focused ones, like flank steak with chimichurri sauce.

Desserts have to be ordered at the same time as the rest of your meal. Each is prepared to order, and the options include a number of things that won't keep, including the perennial molten chocolate cake and more original warm tarts. The menu is always changing, so put your waiters to the test and get their opinions on the food if you're feeling indecisive.

SECRET
FRANCO-AMERICAN
✤

Woonsocket grew from the mills along its river, and the main source of labor to run them was French Canada. **Union Saint-Jean Baptiste D'Amerique** (68 Cumberland Street, Woonsocket, 334-7773) includes the **Mallet Library** of books, articles, photographs, and other material relating to the French settlement of this area and the rest of the United States — important resources for anyone interested in Franco-American history.

In late August, various groups join for the **Jubile Franco-Americain** (Woonsocket, 724-2200 or 1-800-454-2882, www.tourblackstone.com). It celebrates the French-Canadian contribution to Rhode Island with French music, fiddling, arts, and culture.

SECRET
FREE MUSIC
✤

From early music to a new composition making its debut, and from jazz to a soprano solo, you're likely to find it at free recitals and performances held at area colleges. Don't expect amateurs. The **Brown University Jazz Band** (863-3234) and the **Providence College Early Music Ensemble** are but two of the groups to be heard. The best source of information is the "Live This Weekend" section of the *Providence Journal* or the listings in the *Providence Phoenix*. Other free musical performances include the **Blackstone Valley Heritage Concert Series** (722-7934), held in Pawtucket churches.

SECRET GALLERIES

It's not that the **Providence Art Club** (11 Thomas Street, 331-1114) is hiding — it's pretty hard to hide a building that looks like it was built in the Middle Ages, unless you're in a medieval European city, of course. You just don't expect such a building, nor the pink house next door (also built in the 1700s), to contain contemporary art. The pink house with the suspended doorway (the entry was raised to create a shop on the street floor) was the home of the jeweler who invented — or at least perfected — the process of gold plating and founded the costume jewelry industry. Both galleries are open to the public and free.

The **Sarah Doyle Gallery** (Sarah Doyle Women's Center, 185 Meeting Street, 863-2189), at Brown University, specializes in showcasing the work of local artists. Across the river in Downcity, **Center City Artisans** (The Arcade, 65 Weybosset Street, 521-2990) promotes the work of Rhode Island artists. Also in Downcity, **AS220** (115 Empire Street, 831-9327) has two art galleries, a performance space, and a cafe.

At **Helianthus** (398 Wickenden Street, 421-4390), artist Loren Chen adds the work of fellow Rhode Island School of Design pottery artists to his own strikingly colored art pottery. About half the work is his, and other fine local crafts add variety to the upbeat shop.

SECRET GAME GEEKS
✦

For those to whom the following cryptic words have meaning, read on: Warhammer; Magic: The Gathering; AD&D; Werewolf: The Apocalypse; GURPS... **Your Move Games** (752 North Main Street, 455-2300) is a gaming store for those who like their games to include role playing, the battle between good and evil, or little metal figures moved around facsimile battlegrounds (note that these games do not include many historical ones; the focus is more on the SF and fantasy set). The store hosts tournaments on its great big gaming tables in a warehouse atmosphere, livened up by posters of warrior robots and forces of evil that must be destroyed, and — of course — a vending machine stocked with caffeinated sodas. The selection of minis approaches comprehensive, at least when the store isn't waiting for an order to arrive. The book stock can get sparse between deliveries, especially White Wolf materials. Naturally, Your Move is a good place to advertise for players if you want to run a campaign of any sort, or to find a game if you are new in town and want to meet people with whom you have something in common.

SECRET GARDENS
✦

Many of the townhouses that line Benefit Street have gardens you can see over low fences. However, you can enjoy a few of these gardens at closer range, walking through or pausing to sit amid their flowers. The **Stephen Hopkins House**, at the corner of Hopkins Street (Benefit Street, at Hopkins Street, 751-1758), is the restored home of Rhode Island's preeminent statesman of the Revolutionary War period. You can visit the modest residence free of charge (Wednesdays and Saturdays, 1 PM to 4 PM, April to mid-December), but you can stroll through its garden any time by just opening the gate, which sticks a bit but isn't locked. Built in terraces, the garden overlooks the shining gold dome of a former banking hall backed by the modern skyline — a perfect picture of colonial Benefit Street flowing gently into modern Downcity. Brick pathways separate parterre beds of herbs and flowers that would have been grown in Hopkins' time, and benches invite you to sit for a moment and savor the view.

On the uphill side of Benefit Street, at the corner of College Street, is a pair of hillside gardens, one on either side of the red brick **Truman Beckwith House** (42 College Street). The smaller front flower garden faces two streets, its luxuriance restrained by an ornamental iron fence. Follow the walkway around the front of the house to discover the steep terraces of a larger garden, step after step of flowers and shrubs rising to a small garden house. Flowering dogwood decorates it in the spring and a succession of blooms highlights the greenery throughout the season. The garden is open any time and cast-iron chairs on the flagstone terrace provide a place to sit.

A third garden is half a block downhill from Benefit Street, behind **Shakespeare's Head** (21 Meeting Street, 831-7440). The building was, in the 1700s, a bookstore of that name, as well as a print shop for the *Providence Gazette*. Behind the house is a charming sunken garden, bordered by lilacs and shaded by the spreading limbs of an apple tree. Bring a picnic lunch here, as locals who work in adjacent

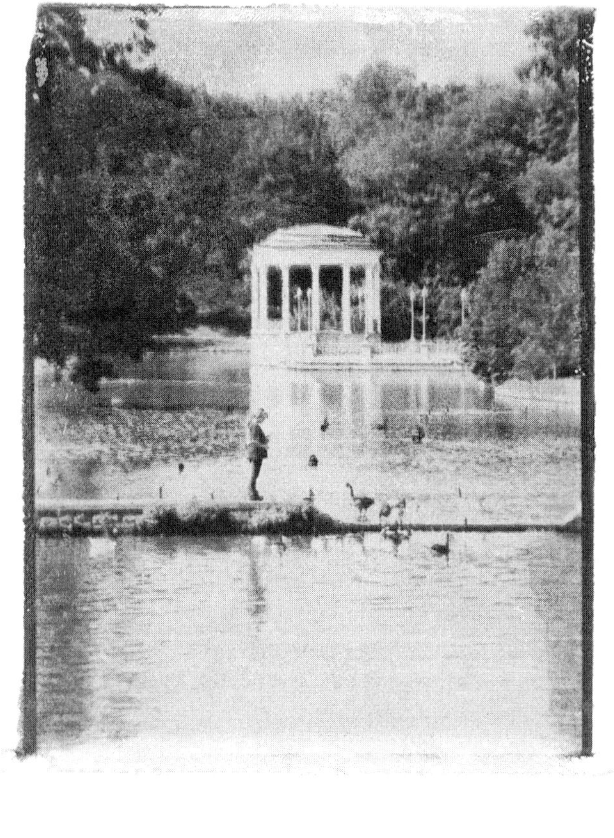

buildings do. Or stop in after dark, when the garden is bathed in light from no obvious source — very charming. The building houses the Providence Preservation Society (see "Secret Guides").

SECRET
GAY AND LESBIAN
✤

A pizza parlor opposite the site of George M. Cohan's birthplace in a Portuguese neighborhood isn't the first place I'd look for a gay-friendly hangout, but then I'm straight, so what do I know? **The Castro** (77 Ives Street, at Wickenden Street, 421-1144) makes some wonderful pizzas, both traditional and exotic (hearts of palm pizza?), and serves all comers cheerily. Despite the palm trees on the awning, the "Castro" it's named for is in San Fran, not Cuba — wink, wink — and the crowd is a mix of gay, lesbian, and straight, including neighborhood kids running in and out for sodas and after-school slices. For me, it has been a great place to sit with a book and watch the world go by while avoiding reading social theory. There are some tasty sweet treats for afternoon snacking. The Castro doubled its dining room space in the summer of 2001, making room for a nice performance space and assuring me the place will stick around for a while to come.

SECRET
GIFTS
❖

To be honest, I've bought very few gifts at **The Goodie Basket** (780 Hope Street, 273-1667). I mean to, but things I get there just keep popping into my mouth, which makes them unfit for later presentation. Everything in this elegantly designed shop is chosen for its suitability as a gift basket ingredient, although any of the goodies would make nice small gifts on their own. Packages of tea cookies and the fine teas to go with them, colorful candy sticks in interesting flavors, and the crème-de-la-crème of jams, preserves, and condiments are set off by a few non-food additions. You can walk around and collect things, which the owners will arrange beautifully for you, or you can call and ask them to create a basket for you. Or you can treat it, as I do, as your own private indulgence and nip in for a bag of chocolate-coated cranberries whenever temptation strikes.

SECRET
GREENS
❖

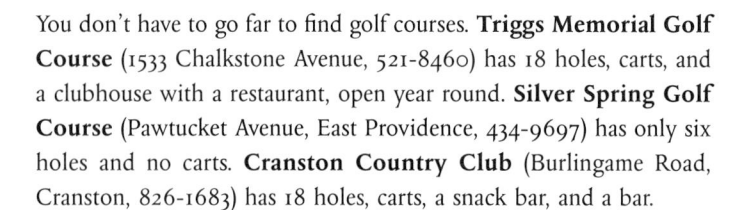

You don't have to go far to find golf courses. **Triggs Memorial Golf Course** (1533 Chalkstone Avenue, 521-8460) has 18 holes, carts, and a clubhouse with a restaurant, open year round. **Silver Spring Golf Course** (Pawtucket Avenue, East Providence, 434-9697) has only six holes and no carts. **Cranston Country Club** (Burlingame Road, Cranston, 826-1683) has 18 holes, carts, a snack bar, and a bar.

SECRET
GUIDES
✧

To see the enormous range of the city's architectural largesse, begin at the **Providence Preservation Society** (21 Meeting Street, 831-7440) and choose one or more of its excellent neighborhood guides. Well illustrated and knowledgeably written, they describe neighborhoods of particular architectural interest, with maps and pointers for identifying styles. They lead to parts of the city far off the main routes, such as Broadway, Elmwood, and the Armory District. Other booklets cover Benefit Street, Downtown, and Brown University in detail.

SECRET
HIGH CHURCH
✧

Episcopalians of an Anglican persuasion can take comfort in knowing that **St. Stephen's Church** (114 George Street, 421-6702) is a bulwark of High Churchness in New England. Sung Mass is celebrated every Sunday, when the choir is accompanied by an organ of 75 ranks of pipes. For those less concerned with ecclesiastical issues, St. Stephen's is notable for several other reasons. Among a considerable collection of outstanding stained glass, it possesses a Tiffany window and another by the Tiffany studio. Another work of art worth locating is the St. Nicholas relief, over the font, a 12th-century Italian piece carved of alabaster. To the left of the high altar, on the St. Stephen's altar, is an exquisite altarpiece of 15th-century painted panels.

SECRET HIPPOS
※

Dalrymple Boathouse (Roger Williams Park, Elmwood Avenue, 785-3510) rents pedal boats, several of which are shaped and painted like hippos. The boathouse is easy to spot: it's the half-timbered building at the water's edge, with a round tower.

SECRET HOLY HOSTELRY
※

I am not recommending you enter the **Sportsman's Inn** (122 Fountain Street, 751-1133) — or warning you off, either — because I haven't been there to see their exotic dancers, or to judge the quality of their hotel rooms with special adult entertainment on the TVs. What I do recommend is standing on the opposite side of the street and reading the ironic inscription on the building lintel, running the length of the facade. It makes me giggle every time. I think it was built as a YMCA in its first life, and the holy intentions remain in spite of its sinful modern purpose.

SECRET HORSES
✤

You've probably seen the snazzy-looking mounted police in Providence, but did you know you could visit them at home? The **Mounted Command Building** (Roger Williams Park, 785-9450) houses the stables for the city's equine police cruisers and you can take a free tour of the facility (between 11 AM and 2 PM, Monday to Thursday).

To ride a horse, head for another huge park, Lincoln Woods. This state park surrounds Olney Pond in Lincoln, and you can reach it from Route 146 or Route 123 (Breakneck Hill Road). **Sunset Stables** (off Route 146, 722-3033) is near the park's western entrance and offers trail rides through Lincoln Woods on weekday afternoons or all day on Saturdays and Sundays. The stables close an hour before sunset and are open year round.

SECRET HOUSES
✤

The **Festival of Historic Houses**, sponsored by the Providence Preservation Society (831-7440), is held in mid-June, when gardens are at their peak of bloom. Tickets are often sold out for this rare chance to see inside private homes of particular architectural or historic interest, so an early reservation is essential.

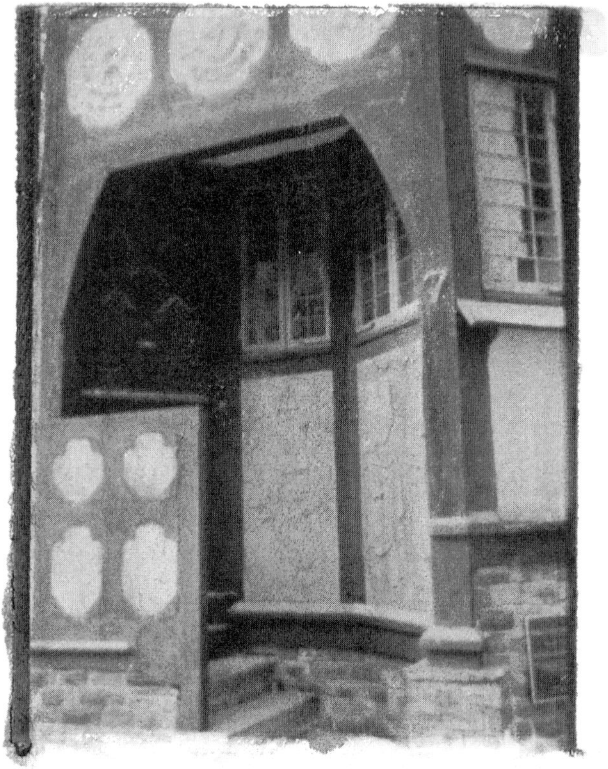

Early in December, East Greenwich holds its **Annual Luminaria Candlelight Tour** (885-0020) of historic buildings and private homes. This is often the only time these interiors are on public view. Many of them are also good examples of historic preservation, useful to those restoring their own homes.

SECRET
H.P. LOVECRAFT
⚜

Funny thing. Both H.P. Lovecraft and E.A. Poe — the seminal masters of the Gothic horror tale — lived in Providence. Does that say something about the effect the city has on sensitive minds? Lovecraft has the stronger claim — he was a native and used Providence as a setting for his tales. His own setting for eternity is **Swan Point Cemetery** (585 Blackstone Boulevard, 272-1314), under a stone that reads simply, "I am Providence." The day to visit it, I discovered quite by accident, is March 15. Let me tell you how I know. One March Sunday, when I was finishing my master's thesis, it was too convincingly about-to-be-spring and I wanted some fresh air. I decided on a walk in the cemetery, easily persuaded my mate to join me, and off we went — flannel shirts, dirty hair, and all.

We walked around, searching vaguely for Lovecraft's grave (on weekdays, the office will give you a booklet listing the locations of all the famous people). We had started back toward the entrance when a car full of romantically gothed-up 20-somethings drove up. One of the occupants said, "Hey, do you guys know... nah, you wouldn't," and drove off. What was that supposed to mean? (Ironically, we ourselves wear goth clothing more often than not — just not to study in). We continued up the main drive toward the exit gate, in time to witness a young man with bleached white hair, bowler hat, long black coat, ruffled shirt, vest, and watch fob stride through the gate, walking stick keeping pace with his progress. Hmm, we thought, something must be up. So we decided to shadow him. If anyone knows where Lovecraft's grave is, it's gotta be him. After much clever evasion and dodging between gravestones, we came across the following tableau.

Our haberdashed guide entered a semi-circle of the faithful and their arcane implements. A sword and dagger leaned against a large simple gravestone; a cut-crystal bottle of dark liquid (wine, of course) sat at their tips; and more than one person held a book. Introductions seemed to be made, then conversation. From behind our gravestone, we got kinda bored at this point. That had to be *the* grave, but we were too shy to go asking questions (we were also a little nervous that we might be sacrificed to Cthulhu — Lovecraft's big, nasty, octopus-like demon god). So we snuck away to do some research into the life of Lovecraft, and learned that that very day was the 60th anniversary of the horror-meister's demise. Providence was not, in fact, consumed by dark forces that day, and — Plunderdome notwithstanding — is still on the grow. So we have to assume, against our more active imaginations, that this was the meeting of an Internet-based Lovecraft fan group, who agreed to meet at his grave in person to mark the death of their hero with the trappings of his age.

Lovecraft-ophiles will find his papers — more than 2,000 of his letters and 3,000 more he received from correspondents — and a collection of his writings that includes nearly 300 original manuscripts, at Brown University's John Hay Library (see "Secret Rare Books"). On the library's front lawn, a monument commemorates the centenary of

Lovecraft's birth. Like Poe, he spent a lot of time at the Providence Athenaeum (see "Secret Edgar Allen Poe").

SECRET
ICE

In the center of the city is a year-round outdoor rink twice the size of Rockefeller Center's. The **Fleet Skating Center** (Kennedy Plaza) provides ice skating from late October through March and roller skating the rest of the year. Skate rentals and lessons are available. Ponds at Roger Williams Park (Elmwood Avenue, 785-3510) become scenic skating rinks in the winter, with a warming shelter at the Dalrymple Boat House.

SECRET
ICE CREAM

Crisis struck Thayer Street when **Maximillian's Ice Cream** (1074 Hope Street, 273-2736) closed its shop there. Perhaps it was the B&J's down the street. Now fans have to drive to the Pawtucket line to get their favorite scoops. It's only five minutes, and it's worth it not only to taste the ice cream, but also to support a local business. Maximillian's flavors come in three tiers of extravagance, differently priced. Sundaes and toppings are above the ordinary in variety and quality. Flavors change daily, but some you might find are raspberry truffle, green tea, or my favorite, just plain maple. Try it as a maple milkshake. The shop is big with lots of seats and good atmosphere for sharing a malted with your sweetie. There's always a stack of the *Providence Phoenix* by the door, so you can figure out where to dance off that banana split you just polished off.

SECRET ITALIAN

Federal Hill, through the center of which runs Atwells Avenue, has traditionally been Providence's Italian neighborhood. Although a few other things may have crept in, it's still pretty solidly Italian. You know you're there when you pass through an arch over the street with a giant pine cone. Caffes, food emporia, restaurants, and the three-layer fountain in Piazza Pasquale leave no question as to the area's ethnicity. In fact, in places, you could be fooled into thinking you were in Italy, especially inside some of the food shops. During the weekend closest to Columbus Day, a festival brings everyone to Federal Hill to enjoy street entertainers and sidewalk stalls along Atwells Avenue. A Sunday parade crowns the weekend (see "Secret Cop Clown").

Venda Ravioli (265 Atwells Avenue, 421-9105) makes fresh mozzarella and sausage and is a center for anything connected with Italian food.

For dinner on Federal Hill, I head to **L'Epicurio** (238 Atwells Avenue, 454-8430) for one of the chef's half-dozen daily entrees.

The seasonal menu will almost always include a veal dish, and certainly at least one seafood selection. I forgo the pasta course and begin with a mascarpone polenta, redolent of sun-dried tomatoes and wild mushrooms.

But the biggest Italian secret is Knightsville. This good-sized Cranston neighborhood is populated almost entirely by immigrants from a single Italian town. Two restaurants face each other across Cranston Street, each with its partisans, but both almost equally good. My own preference is **L'Osteria** (1703 Cranston Street, Cranston, 943-3140), with very few tables, a knockout menu, and some of the finest swordfish I've ever tasted. Presentation is an art here, and in this intimate atmosphere, where everyone looks to see what's being brought to the neighboring table, diners are likely to end up in a culinary discussion with total strangers. Lunches are excellent, too, but only served Tuesday through Saturday. The larger **Caffe Itri** (1686 Cranston Street, Cranston, 942-1970) also has an excellent menu, featuring a wide range of Italian cooking styles.

SECRET JUNGLE

On a wintry day, when I need a quick trip to the tropics but have to be back in time for dinner, I head for the Brown University Plant Environment Center's **Conservatory** (Waterman Street, between Thayer and Prospect streets), where a steaming warm jungle grows inside a glass house. Green is everywhere: delicate little African violets face a begonia with shiny green leaves the size of turkey platters, and a hand of little green bananas that never seem to ripen hangs overhead. Trees push against the glass ceiling, and in one corner is a prickly lot of cacti. All the plants are arranged by their botanical families. There are upwards of 10,000 species in this and adjacent greenhouses. The conservatory is open until 3:30 PM.

SECRET KINK

❖

Got an itch to scratch? Need some action? On rather rundown North Main Street, heading toward Pawtucket, keep an eye on the right side of the street for **Miko Exoticwear** (653 North Main Street, 421-6646). The windows will assure you that you've found it — unlike seedy sex-shops, Miko is proud to tell the world that the store loves PVC, leather, vinyl, lace, and stiletto heels, and to show passersby what inner hottie potential they could have in the right outfit. Outfits range from quality "naughty nurse" role-playing costumes to elegant corsetry. Designers include Stormy Leather, out of San Francisco, and Catherine Coatney, who creates starkly tailored evening wear. Miko is a good spot to hunt for goth club wear as well as fetish wear. The store is sure to have a dazzling array of fishnet stockings in every form and color, as well as some excellent shiny, shiny leather boots and plenty of black anything.

Kink is more than the outfit, of course. Miko carries risqué — but socially acceptable — Kama Sutra brand products, like honey dust and heavenly scented lotions, along with more scandalous restraints, metal clips and clamps, and adult toys for every orifice. The store sponsors fetish nights at clubs in Providence, so stop by and ask what's on the schedule, or pick up a copy of the *Providence Phoenix* for club listings.

SECRET
LABOR DAY

It's about the only place I know that has a really bang-up — and very appropriate — celebration of Labor Day. The venue is appropriate, too, since if any place can claim to be the spot where America's Industrial Revolution began, it's the Slater Mill. The **Rhode Island Labor and Ethnic Heritage Festival** (Slater Mill, Pawtucket, 724-2200 or 1-800-454-2882, www.tourblackstone.com) celebrates working men and women of the Blackstone Valley and their diversity of cultural and ethnic traditions. Art, history, and labor themes blend into a day of fun for all ages, with live performances, folk singing, and storytelling. The entertainment and exhibits may be Irish, French, Cambodian, Native American, African, bluegrass, or Hispanic — or all of these. Labor unions, service organizations, and craftsmen all join in creating lively displays, and riverboat excursions carry visitors back into the area's industrial history. The **Slater Mill** (see "Secret Revolution") is open for tours all day and there's plenty of food available.

SECRET
LEAF PEEPING
※

When the maples are their red and orange best, the **Fall Foliage Train Excursion**, run by the Blackstone Valley Tourism Council (724-2200 or 1-800-454-2882, www.tourblackstone.com), puts you where the color is. The train leaves Cumberland at 10 AM and travels on the old Providence and Worcester line to Worcester, Massachusetts, returning at 2 PM. Bring a picnic lunch or buy it on board. Seats sell out, so reserve early.

To see even more colored leaves, and some pretty mill towns as well, follow the **Self-Drive Foliage Tour** (724-2200 or 1-800-454-2882, www.tourblackstone.com) through Chepachet, Pascoag, and Harrisville, and along the Blackstone Valley. The route travels through some lovely Rhode Island countryside and towns, all clearly mapped by the Blackstone Valley Tourism Council — a good source of information on the entire area north of Providence.

SECRET
LEGS AND EGGS
※

Contemplate the notion. Friday mornings between 6 AM and 11 AM, you can go to the **Foxy Lady Club** (318 Chalkstone Avenue, 331-9145) and have a full hearty American breakfast while watching exotic dancers. This seems so very bizarre to me — aren't strip clubs a social outing kind of place? What circumstances would lead anyone to wake up early enough to go for this hedonistic *early morning* indulgence, when they could sleep in? Is this something workin' guys do to inaugurate the last day of the work week? ("Aw, honey, I got a morning meeting Friday, don't bother to wake up and make me breakfast.") Or is this a haunt of night-shift policemen and firemen just off duty? Frat boys after all-night binges? Or a constant parade of curiosity-seekers like me and my friends?

SECRET
LIFE EXPECTANCY CLOCK
✤

Power freaks and bean counters who need to plan things down to the last detail will appreciate this convenient accessory for their mantel. You can buy one for yourself or a loved one at **Copacetic Rudely Elegant Jewelry** (The Arcade, 65 Weybosset Street, 273-0470), along with handy-dandy little trinkets like poison rings.

SECRET
LLAMAS
✤

They're such ungainly beasts, and so unlike any of our native animals, that they never fail to fascinate people. On Sunday afternoons, **The Llama Farma** (Cumberland, 334-1873) offers family hikes or longer adult hikes, with the llamas carrying your lunch. The farm also does sunset hikes, with wine and cheese served. One llama accompanies every two people on these hikes. You can also watch when their wool is being sheared.

SECRET LORT

Hah, gotcha! Bet you don't know what lort is. It's a chewy noodle-dumpling sort of thing that comes tossed with vegetables or meat at **Apsara** (716 Public Street, 785-1490). It has a subtle toasted flavor, and an intense chewiness that makes it very satisfying and warming on a cold night. Of course, the southeast Asian menu has a number of other treats for other moods. A hot-weather favorite that awakens my wilted appetite is the platter of fresh cool noodles, sprouts, herbs, plantain, greens, and other vegetables that you wrap into fresh softened rice paper sheets and eat with dipping sauce. Rice noodle sheets are brought to your table dry, along with a bowl of hot water — dip the sheets in one at a time, just for a few seconds, until they go limp. Line up your choice of fillings along the center, fold the ends over to cover the filling, and roll up snugly. The folded ends should hold the filling inside, and the slight stickiness of the wrapper should hold the roll shut. Dip an end in the sauce, bite it off, and repeat until done. For best results, don't overfill your roll — they will bring you more wrappers if you need them. The restaurant is rather popular, despite its out-of-the-way location, so you may have to wait for a table. It is not fancy — Formica tables and booth seating, some paintings on the wall and a Buddhist altar by the door for decoration,

and service on the slow and overworked side on weekend nights —
but it's worth it. And the informal atmosphere means you can go there
no matter how dressed up or down you happen to be.

SECRET
MANDOO
❧

Tucked around a corner off Wickenden Street, **Café Yuni** (10
Traverse Street, 272-3585) is easy to miss. Even when you see the
awning, it seems unlikely that such a tiny corner could really be the
front of a restaurant. It has six tables — fewer if the servers have to
push them together for larger parties. The seating area in front of the
sushi bar is always unusable because things have been piled up there.
The TV is always on, usually showing golf. But the homestyle Korean
cooking can't be beat, not in the whole city.

Is it cold outside, so cold it's in your bones? Try the ultimate Korean
comfort food, born of millennia of winters on the Korean peninsula
— mandoo-gok, a clear broth flavored with invigorating ginger and
scallion, with two kinds of dumplings bobbing in it.

Is it so hot and sticky that you've lost your appetite? Revive it with
lunchbox trays: compartments of spicy kimchee, juicy spinach salad,
crispy thick bean sprouts, and succulent beef that will lure you to eat.
The cafe serves several types of bi-bim-bap, including some in scalding
stone bowls — the correct way to eat it is to immediately break the
egg with your chopsticks and stir it in, so the stone will cook everything together. By the end of your meal, you have to pull toasted bits
of food from the inside of the bowl. It is bad form to leave even a

single grain of rice in your dish, but not because it's impolite; it's the notion of wastefulness that most bothers at least one waitress here, who exhorted a friend of mine to finish everything before she said she was through. The restaurant is immaculate, casual, and host to a steady flow of Korean students from the Rhode Island School of Design and Brown University, and a good number of others enamored of its food. By the way, the scallion pancakes . . . yummmmmmm . . .

SECRET MANSIONS
※

Several of Providence's finest old mansions are preserved and open to the public — not as museums, but as office buildings for two of the city's colleges. The **Woods Gerry Mansion** (62 Prospect Street, 454-6140) is a splendid Italianate structure of brick, with sandstone trim. Its arching porte-cochere fairly begs you to arrive by carriage. In its youth, it was the largest house in Providence. The house was built on the site of an alarm beacon that sat atop an 85-foot mast; during the Revolution, the beacon warned colonists of approaching British ships. Inside the foyer, you can see changing exhibits from the collections of the Rhode Island School of Design, whose admissions office now occupies the building. Walk around back to see the terrace and the French windows that open onto it. Sculpture decorates the garden. You can see the interior architectural detail Monday through Saturday (10 AM to 4 PM) and Sundays (2 PM to 5 PM).

Brown University has its administrative offices in the **Corliss-Bracket House** (45 Prospect Street, 863-2378), an Italianate villa

MANSIONS

that was the home of inventor George Corliss. His best-known work was the Corliss steam engine, but he also invented the heating and cooling systems for this house. His wife was in frail health, and to ensure her comfort, he devised a climate control mechanism that kept the house at a year-round temperature that never varied by more than one degree. The interior woodwork is elegant, with deep relief carving. Tours of the Brown campus begin here. The building is open weekdays from 9 AM to 5 PM.

SECRET MARINARA
※

In this chic gastronomic new world we live in, Italian restaurants now favor northern and Tuscan specialties, eschewing the Sicilian-based dishes that for generations meant Italian food to Americans. So much so, that there are days when one longs for the good old red-sauce stuff. Thanks to Providence's energetic mayor, Buddy Cianci (of whose doings not much is secret any more), you can create these dishes at home, using a really good recipe, without cutting up all the onions or standing over the sauce. Not your usual out-of-a-jar stuff, **The Mayor's Own Marinara Sauce** is sold all over Federal Hill, and the profits go to scholarships. The sauce, his mother's recipe, was first bottled up as a party favor for a birthday celebration and people wanted more.

Angelo's Civita Farnese (141 Atwells Avenue, 621-8171) makes no pretense to trendy Tuscan cuisine, or to anything else but good old-fashioned Italian-American pasta with red sauce and meat. No one hovers with a bludgeon-sized pepper mill, and you can entertain yourself while waiting for your pasta by feeding quarters into a box to make the model railroad run along its overhead track. Unusually for Federal Hill, Angelo's has parking in back.

SECRET
MOLLUSKS
※

At **Hemenway's** (1 Old Stone Square at South Main Street, 351-8570), you get only the freshest and best oysters and littlenecks, still tasting of the sea. Impeccably fresh fish, whether it's catfish or tuna steak, is served in simple, straightforward ways — often brushed in seasoned butter and grilled, without sauces to interfere with the sea-fresh flavors. The chowder is packed full of chunky shellfish meat.

SECRET
MONASTERY
※

In 1900, a group of Cistercian monks from Nova Scotia established the monastery of Our Lady of the Valley, building a Gothic-style chapel with an octagonal bell tower, clearing the land for farming, and living a contemplative, vegetarian life. **The Monastery** (Route 114 [High Street], Cumberland) ended suddenly when fire destroyed the stone church and damaged the rest of the building. The town now uses the remaining buildings, but the massive stone steps end at the remains of the bell tower, now in Gothic ruin. The garden has been nicely restored, sitting within hedges beside the church ruins.

Trails lead through the property — one to a spot where, many years before the brothers arrived, local Native Americans killed a group of colonists during King Phillip's War.

SECRET NECESSITIES

Public restrooms are available at City Hall and the U.S. District Court (Kennedy Plaza) and in the Garrahy Judicial Complex (91 Dorrance Plaza), all open only on weekdays. Also in Downcity are facilities in the Providence Public Library (225 Washington Street), The Arcade (65 Weybosset Street) and the Amtrak station (100 Gaspee Street). The Traveler's Aid Society (177 Union Street) is open longer hours than the others. On the east side, most Brown University buildings, such as the libraries, have public restrooms.

SECRET NIGHT LIFE

Lupo's Heartbreak Hotel (239 Westminster Street, 272-5876) is the principal venue for known rock groups, rhythm and blues, and jazz. It's a nice environment, too, with an ample lobby area and a connection to the **Met Café** (130 Union Street, 861-2142), with a smaller stage and more intimate atmosphere. The concert-hall setting of the **Veterans Memorial Auditorium** (Brownell Street, 277-3150) hosts, on average, two major performances a month, which have included works from major ballet and opera companies, a choral concert by the Boston Handel and Haydn Society, and shows by top solo musicians. **Stuart Theater** and **Leeds Theater** (Brown University campus, 863-2838) feature larger performances by a wide variety of student groups, as well as guest shows sponsored by campus organizations. Several smaller venues on campus also host student performances. The major alternative theater venue in Providence is the **Perishable Theater Art Center** (95 Empire Street, 331-2695, www.perishable.org). **NewGate Theatre** (134 Mathewson Street, 421-9680, www.newgatetheatre.org) is an intimate loft theater presenting world premieres and some classics. To learn what's in the offing at any of these, check newspaper listings (see "Secret Providence: Introduction").

SECRET PADDLES

Few cities give you the opportunity to kayak safely through the middle of downtown. Until a decade ago the Providence River, which runs through the heart of Downcity, was itself a secret. Its entire lower section was covered by a bridge so solid that few people who drove over it daily knew that water flowed underneath it. But when Providence uncovered the river and its residents rediscovered it, they embraced it with enthusiasm.

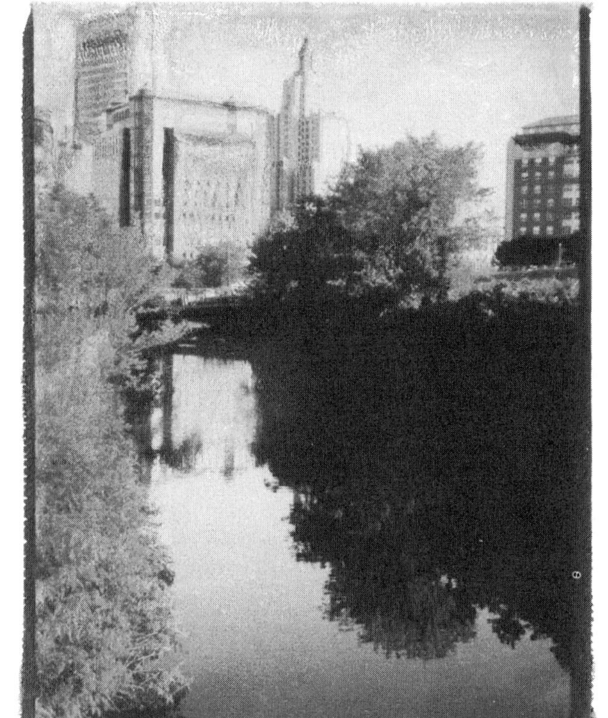

Locals and visitors stroll its promenade, sip wine and coffee in cafes that overlook it, bring picnic lunches to its grassy banks, and hold festivals around it. They even light it with bonfires during periodic WaterFire evenings.

People with their own kayaks began paddling in its waters, and now you can rent these craft right at the river. Paddle about on your own, take lessons, or join a group to explore this and other local rivers. **Paddle Providence** (22 Water Street, 453-1633, www.paddleprovidence.org) rents single sea kayaks for about $30 a day, and doubles or canoes for $35 a day. You can reserve a kayak ahead of time, or just stop by and take your chances.

The Blackstone River offers good kayaking and canoeing from Pawtucket north, along almost its entire length. There is a put-in at the Slater Mill Historic Site, which you can reach from the parking area next to the mill. **Friends of the Blackstone** (contact Leon Kowal, 766-6262) was formed to protect and clean up the river, and to educate the public about its history and environment. The group's volunteers aim to restore the river and its banks as close as possible to a natural state. Along with cleaning up the river, they are trying to restore fishing by stocking trout in the spring and fall and by building fish ladders. They also offer canoe lessons — including special lessons for kids at a local pool — and guided canoe explorations of the river. You can use your own canoe or borrow one from the group's fleet of 22.

The **Blackstone Heritage Council** (Blackstone River Valley National Heritage Corridor, 762-0440) also offers paddling programs, including a 14-week **Paddle Tuesday** series in the summer. The biggest event of the year for paddlers is the **Woonsocket Riverfest**, which features a 4.2-mile race in May, when paddlers compete in several classes. The race begins at River Island Park, and a shuttle service is offered for canoes and paddlers.

SECRET
PAGAN BIKE RENTALS
※

Esta's Too (257 Thayer Street, 831-3651) is a weird little spot. You can buy whatever dorm-room decor is the rage of the month there, along with a smattering of neo-pagan books and supplies. But they also rent videos and bikes, which comes in very handy on a nice day, with a beautiful bike path a 10-minute pedal away. Take a ride, return the bike, pick up a movie, go home and veg out knowing you've earned your right to lethargy that night. For bikes, go to the alley between Esta's and the Indian restaurant next door. Trust me, they're back there.

The **East Bay Bike Path** borders Narragansett Bay as far as Bristol, and a bike path follows the river through India Point Park to extend the bike route right into Downcity Providence. **Roger Williams Park**, north of town, has miles of paved roadways and paths, and offers welcome shade for summer bikers. Newly opened along the upper reaches of the historic Blackstone Canal is a 3.5-mile bike path, part of **Blackstone River State Park** (Lincoln, 222-4203, ext. 4042, www.riparks.com). Expect this path to grow to a full 19 miles, between Pawtucket and the Massachusetts border.

SECRET PAGODA
✤

The **Providence Zen Center** (99 Pound Road, Cumberland, 658-1464) is actually located in Cumberland. That makes it all the better for peaceful meditation and organic gardening, at a site that includes a spacious and airy meditation hall and a towering pagoda. I stumbled on the center while seeking out organic farm stands, and when I saw the pagoda I had to stop. The place was silent. Inside the lovely hall is a seated Buddha surrounded by lotuses and accoutrements, sun pouring through a skylight illuminating his gilded serenity. The pagoda sits at the front of the complex, a classic form of Buddhist architecture consisting of tier upon tier of upturned roofs built around a central pillar. (This form of construction explains why there are still so many ancient pagodas standing in earthquake-ridden places such as Japan. Construction around a single pole allows the structure some flexibility to bend under stress, instead of ripping apart the way a structure based on four corner posts does.)

The Providence Zen Center is the international head temple for the Kwan Um School of Zen, a Korean form of the ascetic sect that stresses meditation and development of a community of followers through practice and time spent together. The center also supports interfaith activities like frequent Christian-Buddhist retreats. There's a schedule of regular practice sessions, and a gift shop sells supplies for practitioners as well as a few local products — honey, and candy made by a nearby Trappist convent. The center welcomes quiet and respectful visitors who will look around discreetly.

SECRET
PAPAYA
✤

On a quest to visit every diner in Rhode Island (the diner was "born" in Providence, after all), I stopped by **Roberto's Diner** (777 Elmwood Avenue, 461-7770) one wintry Sunday afternoon with my S.O. A beautiful old diner car in excellent condition, it had been a soul-food diner until recently, so I was surprised to see "Dominican Specialties" advertised on the sign outside. As we opened the door, the soundtrack to *The Matrix* flooded over us so strongly that my ribs vibrated. A guy on a stool and a guy behind the counter were watching the movie, showing on a screen over the counter, but the employee welcomed us cheerily. I peered at the menu of Dominican dishes, and asked him what a batida was. "It's like a milkshake," he said. "You'll like it." I tried a papaya one. Half an hour later, we finally left, having ordered another batida and watched the grand finale to *The Matrix* with sound quality no movie theater could improve on. Their sound system is amazing. The batida specialist told me they are open after the clubs get out, and people come here to meet their late-night munching needs and wind down with some hot Latin music. I imagine the club sound systems must pale in comparison, since the old arch-topped diner has acoustics I never dreamed of.

And the batidas started an obsession for us. Based on watching our diner friend make our second one, and a consultation with a Cuban cookbook, I figured out the very simple recipe — papaya pulp, evaporated milk from a can, an ice cube or two, and sweetener, blended until frothy. But papayas are expensive in New England, so this was a costly little treat . . . until I discovered the canned papaya at **Ocean State Job Lot** (361 Reservoir Avenue, 461-1181). For under a dollar a can, I got papaya cubes in sugar syrup, which come close enough to the fresh thing to make me happy. With a touch of the packing syrup for the sweetener, a can makes two big batidas. Job Lot also has God-Alone-Knows-what-else — I've found Adidas baby socks here, and a set of espresso cups and plates that looked fresh off the Left Bank for a mere $5. It's all close-outs, overstock, and whatnot, and there's no telling what you'll find, but chances are it will be cheap and fill some need you hadn't fully realized you had.

SECRET PARK
⚜

India Point Park is on the waterfront on the east side (not to be confused with the separate East Providence), on the site of John Brown's piers and warehouses, which made Providence a major port in the China Trade. This small park has sailing access and a children's playground. In the summer, it is the site of the Waterfront Festival.

SECRET PARKING
⚜

Many Downcity lots and garages offer early-bird specials on all-day parking before 9 AM. The largest downtown parking garage is on Eddy Street, behind the Biltmore Hotel. There is a large garage at the

Amtrak station, near Waterplace Park, and there are two lots behind Old Union Station, on Memorial Boulevard. Three more are on Pine Street, which parallels Weybosset behind the Johnson and Wales University campus, and there are several more on Weybosset and Westminster streets. On Frances Street, close to the Veterans Memorial Auditorium, is a 600-car facility.

SECRET PARROTS

No, they aren't in a pet shop or at the zoo. They live in big unruly nests that give new perspective to a bad hair day, and they line up along the telephone wires of **Sabin Point** like rows of oversized green clothespins.

This otherwise quiet and un-exotic residential neighborhood is in the Crescent Point section of East Providence, just before the town line of Barrington. Drive past the carousel (see "Secret Carousels") and bear left into Sabin Point. As you circle the point, you will see the parrots and — especially when the leaves are off the trees — their untidy nests. The birds fly between trees or rest on branches, wires, and fences, and are quite easy to spot. Evidently, a flock stopped here after being blown off course during its annual migration and adapted to the New England winter.

PARROTS 85

SECRET
PASTA

The Pasta Challenge (351-6440) in September is an all-you-can-eat extravaganza pitting pasta against pasta in a friendly rivalry among local restaurant chefs. You'll get to sample some outstanding dishes and vote for the best pasta creations. The competition is strong, since Providence has an abundance of Italian restaurants.

For pasta made in-house, which you can buy to cook at home or consume on the spot, go to **Rachel's Pastanova** (71 Hope Street, 351-8585). Rachel's inspirations for ingredients come from all over the world. On her shelves may be Thai, Jamaican, or other exotic flavors, and at the pasta bar you can design your own dish. Choose the flavor or color of pasta and embellish it with ingredients chosen from a long, long list that includes pesto, sun-dried tomatoes, olives, scallops, and vegetables.

SECRET
PAWSOX

Baseball season runs from early April through August for the AAA Red Sox farm team, the **Pawtucket Red Sox** (McCoy Stadium, Columbus Avenue at South Bend and Division streets, Pawtucket, 724-7300, www.pawsox.com). A full schedule of lively hometown-team baseball is planned so that there are one or more games during most weeks of the season. The stadium opens two hours before game time, and carry-in food or beverages aren't allowed. Tickets for handicapped accessible seats are available in advance at the ticket office at the stadium. All tickets will remind your parents of baseball prices when they were kids.

SECRET PORTUGUESE
✥

East Providence — the part of town over the red bridge — is the heart and soul of Portuguese Providence. But you'll find many other places that reflect the influence of this significant ethnic population and its culture. My favorite is **Friends Market** (126 Brook Street, 861-0435) and I almost listed it under "Secret Cheese," because it's the only place apart from some little farms in the Serra de Estrella where I can get real Portuguese mountain cheese. Not only the cheese, but also wonderful terra-cotta pottery dishes to serve it on.

Follow Hope Street north until it meets Route 114 in Pawtucket, then follow Route 114 through Central Falls to find the **Valley Park Cervezaria** (17 Mill Street, at Broad Street [Route 114], Cumberland, 723-4490). A *cervezaria* is a beer joint, in its closest translation, but in Portugal (and here) it means not a dive, but a friendly cafe/restaurant where neighbors gather in the evening over coffee, a glass of vinho verde, or a beer. This little cafe rarely sees out-of-towners in its bar or in its separate dining room, where the daily special might be the delicious pork Alentejo style with freshwater clams or a mammoth bowl of shellfish swimming in a rich, steaming broth. Our whole family chose this unlikely spot for dinner one Easter Sunday and you can imagine our collective delight to find that the day's special was roast suckling pig.

Within sight is the more upscale but equally welcoming **Serra d'Estrella** (168 Broad Street, Valley Falls, 725-9597). Start with a steaming bowl of caldo verde and move on to shrimp (gambas) or one of several cod (baccalau) dishes. The wine list includes some of the best Portuguese wines. On weekend nights, a singer usually performs Portuguese music at **Lisboa a Noite** (17 Exchange Street, Pawtucket, 723-2035). Seafood specialties lead the menu: lobster in spicy green cilantro sauce and Alentejo-style pork are both good choices.

The **Cape Verdean Independence Day Celebration** (India Point Park, India Street, 222-4133) is in July, with events for the whole family reflecting this sub-group of Portuguese descendants. Look for food, music, dancing, and a warm welcome.

SECRET
PRANKS

Keep an eye on the statue of Roger Williams, overlooking the city from **Prospect Park** (Congdon Street, at Cushing Street, see "Secret Views") on the east side. He is visible from the Amtrak station. RISD students have a tradition of, er, embellishing him as whimsy dictates. A few years ago he was discovered to have a yoyo dangling from his outstretched hand . . . who can say what it could be next? Even if the merry pranksters aren't active, the park over which Williams presides is a lovely quiet getaway spot for enjoying a picnic or reading a

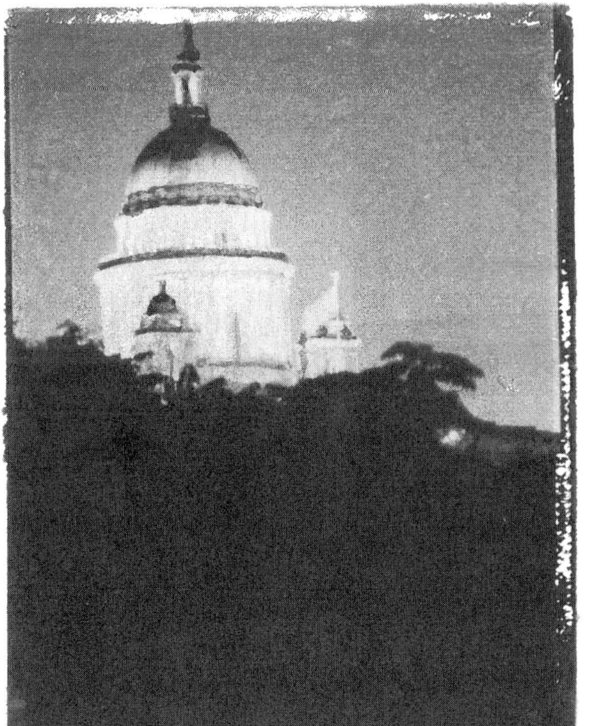

book. The city lies below, sunsets are stunning, and WaterFire is a magically removed spectacle below you from that vantage point. Very romantic.

SECRET
PUBLIC BUILDINGS
⚜

They're buildings we see every day. We may even wander into them to get a document or pay a parking ticket. But we never really tour them.

City Hall (Kennedy Plaza, 421-7740) is a splendid Second Empire-style building (the same style as the Louvre in Paris), restored in the nick of time — just before it either fell down or was knocked down by a wrecking ball. Climb the wide marble stairway to see the upper-floor rooms, especially the richly ornamented council chamber and the aldermen's chamber, with gold stars on its blue ceiling. The two chambers may be locked, which you'd probably rather not discover after you've climbed that long flight of stairs, so ask at the city clerk's office first. If they are locked, a custodian will let you in.

SECRET
RARE BOOKS
⚜

It's hardly news that the **John Hay Library** (20 Prospect Street, 863-2414) is chock-full of rare books, manuscripts, early printed works,

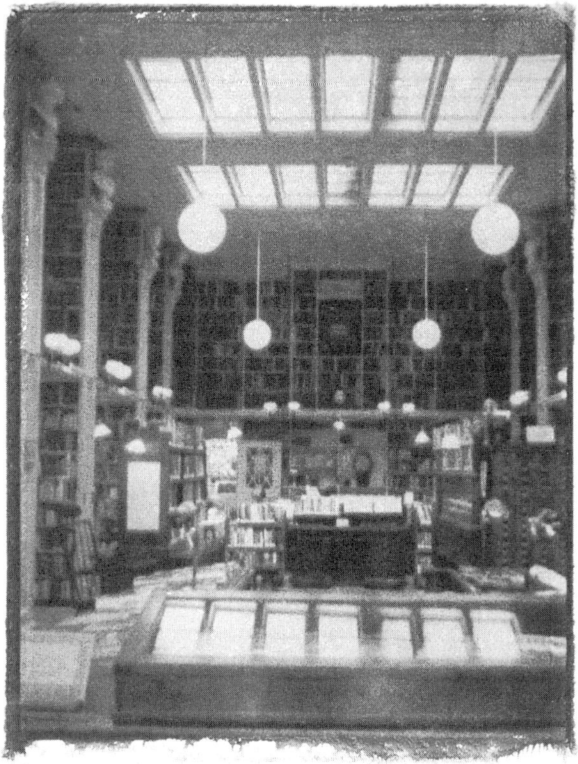

and literary treasures. But deep in its vault is at least one book bound in human skin. "In the 16th and 17th centuries, this was done," a librarian explains, continuing to tell me that the skins were those of convicted criminals, whose remains were not buried in consecrated ground and who were not expected to rise on the Day of Judgment. They're not uncommon in libraries of this ilk, she continued. "Everybody's got one." The one at the Hay Library is a 16th-century book by Andreas Vesalius on, ironically, human anatomy. You need to make an appointment to see it, since it's kept in a climate-controlled vault. Bizarre as this is, it's only an infinitesimal part of the library's interesting holdings, which also include Elizabeth Barrett Browning's tea service and a lock of Napoleon's hair.

SECRET RECIPES

Are you planning a 1940s swing dance party where you want authentic home-front foods to serve? Or would you like to make 1920s tea sandwiches for a ladies' tea, or add authentic Roman foods to your next bacchanal? You'll find the recipes in the archives at Johnson and Wales University, where thousands of books and product advertising pamphlets provide a working culinary history. This library is part of the **Johnson and Wales Culinary Museum** (315 Harborside Boulevard, JWU-2805). The museum is a fascinating, if random, hodgepodge of cooking utensils, chef memorabilia, and other food-related artifacts, spanning 2,000 years of eating and drinking. Tours — the only way to see the assemblage — are uneven. Johnson and

Wales hopes eventually to have a proper home and a curator for the museum, so the collections can be better displayed and professionally interpreted. The museum is off Allen's Avenue, not far from I-95 exit 18. From Allen's Avenue, turn onto Northrup Street, at the Shell station. As you try to find it, you'll think its location is the biggest secret in town.

SECRET REP

The **Trinity Repertory Company** (201 Washington Street, 521-1100) is known for its Tony Award–winning, innovative productions of both classic and contemporary works. It is New England's oldest resident theater company.

SECRET REVOLUTION

Not the American Revolution, but the American Industrial Revolution, began on the banks of the Blackstone River, now preserved as **Slater Mill Historic Site** (Roosevelt Avenue, at Main Street, Pawtucket, 725-8638). The mill sits next to the falls where the Blackstone River drops into tidal waters, its three buildings the sole remnants of a complex of mills that began the fabric manufacturing industry in the United States. If you walk across the impressive double-arched stone bridge, you can look down on the dam that created the first power for the Industrial Revolution, and trace its canals and ditches. In these mills, Samuel Slater designed and built the first of the many machines that broke England's monopoly on spinning thread for cloth. Tours are guided by docents, who will often demonstrate the equipment in the mill, which operated well into living memory.

More industrial archaeology is visible at **Valley Falls Park** (Broad Street [Route 114] at the bridge, Valley Falls, no phone). In 1934, when a large manufacturing company went out of business, Valley Falls was left with acres of deteriorating buildings. Today they form a park, with interpretive panels showing how the mills used water to run the machinery. Walkways lead to parts of the large hydraulic turbine system, providing a look at the complicated water systems that once drove the factories above them. These show part of the process hidden beneath the huge mill complexes that still line many sections of the riverbanks.

SECRET
RHODE ISLANDIANA

The **What Cheer!** antiques shop (5 South Angell Street, 521-5533) is in Myopic Books' basement. A keen appreciation for 20th-century life has driven the owners to pull together an assortment of doodads, from spice canisters to Christmas ornaments, that could be used to reconstruct the sets of "Leave It to Beaver." What Cheer! takes its name from the greeting called out by Rhode Island's founder, Roger Williams, upon meeting a group of native people on the riverbank, where he was about to land and move in with a few followers. It's a downright spiffy name for the store, since it has a good concentration of Rhode Island materials. I pine for their mint Haffenreffer Beer tray, illustrated by Dr. Seuss before the children's market was so good to him. Packaging and advertising products from Rhode Island businesses and industries are well represented, as are travel pamphlets, and coastal maps and charts.

SECRET
RIVERBOAT
✣

The ***Blackstone Valley Explorer*** (724-2200 or 1-800-454-2882, www.tourblackstone.com) is a covered riverboat that tours the Blackstone Valley and Upper Narragansett Bay, interpreting the history and wildlife of the historic waterways. It moves about often, but its schedule is well circulated. The *Explorer* operates from each location for periods ranging from a few days to two weeks. It also does special events, including a Haunted River Tour in October.

SECRET
SAAG
✣

My S.O. and I consider ourselves connoisseurs of saag paneer — cubes of firmly bouncy paneer cheese, delicately flavorful, in a sea of heavenly buttery spinach redolent with ginger, coriander, and cardamom. Our criteria are based on nothing other than what we agree we like. We order saag paneer at every Indian restaurant, we discuss its relative merits with one another, we rank it among its competitors at other places we know. Occasionally we disagree — but on no more than whether there should be more ginger or if they skimped on the clarified butter.

Taste of India (230 Wickenden Street, 421-4355) doesn't serve our favorite saag paneer to date. That is in Boston, and so I can't tell you where. But the saag paneer here is very, very good. Because we feel sheepish about always ordering the same dish, we make our second entree a different one each time. We have consequently sampled most of the menu and deemed it all luscious. The garlic naan is incredible — the garlic just hot, never burned, bursting with flavor that's balanced by copious sprinklings of cilantro. Mango chicken has been on their specials menu for as long as I have been going there — chunks of chicken simmered in a sweetly tangy sauce of puréed mango. They could call it weasel legs in mango sauce and I would order it.

SECRET SAFARI
❖

I got into a shoving match with a grammar-schooler one day at the polar bear habitat at **Roger Williams Park Zoo** (785-3510). You would too, if you could stand at a certain spot in the glass-sided polar bear pool and have the polar bear swim right up to you, meet you face to face, then kick off the wall to head back to the surface. Around and around he swam, in the same circle, bouncing off the same spot on the glass. The little girl stood there, staring into the milky water at the point where the bear became visible, his thick white fur flowing in the currents. She stood her ground, but not without a little thrilled yelp, as he rushed to a glass thickness away, and deflected his huge mass up to the surface, his great big paw going thud where her small hand rested on the glass. It looked like a thrilling adrenaline rush, and I wanted a chance to stand in The Spot and see him coming at me. Her mother didn't see it my way.

The zoo is one of the best in the country, according to some reputable source or another, and I believe it. The animal pens are spacious, with realistic habitats for animals to roam. They do special exhibits, like one on Marco Polo's voyages and the animals he encountered en route — camels, tigers, monkeys, and bears were all penned in an area built to resemble Renaissance sailing vessels and ports of call, with text on the voyages and how the explorers learned about animals wherever they went. This place is definitely above and beyond ordinary zoos. Buildings with contained environments feature exotic birds, and interpreters wander the exhibits helping visitors find all the different creatures lurking in the ecosystem. My favorite is a little bat cave nestled in the exit corridor from the bird habitat, complete with a colony of bats fluttering in the dark. Flashes of sunlight from the door briefly illuminate the realistically modeled bats the zoo has positioned on the ceiling, which make adults jump and children yelp when they see them and think they are real. Trust me, the real bats are well behind glass, and if you stay in there long enough for your eyes to adjust to the darkness, you can see them swooping and diving, and nibbling fruit shish-kebabs left in the cage to feed them.

SECRET
SEWING AND KNITTING

The old mill buildings that once manufactured most of the nation's fabric are silent, and many are vacant or fallen in. But some have been put to new uses as outlet stores with deeply discounted seconds, overruns, and other surplus merchandise. Knitters will find bargains and a large selection of hand-knitting yarns and accessories at **The Yarn Outlet** (280 Rand Street, Central Falls, 722-5600). It is not actually an outlet, but it has very inexpensive yarn, and you can save 30 to 75 percent on knitting supplies and books.

Lorraine Mill Fabrics (593 Mineral Spring Avenue, Pawtucket, 722-9500) is one of the largest fabric stores in the country, always with a wide variety of fabric for sale. This is an off-price outlet, not a manufacturer's outlet. On the east side of the river, **Slater Factory Fabrics** (2 India Road, Cumberland, 727-9068) is a manufacturer's store with decorator fabrics, especially wide ones. Like many other factory stores, it accepts cash only.

Look in the **Ryco Factory Outlet Store** (22 Carrington Street, Lincoln, 725-1779) for ribbons, lace, buttons, and some fabrics. This is a good place for the resourceful bride-to-be to buy wedding accessory makings, such as veiling and lace.

SECRET
SHEETS
✤

Textile Warehouse (111 India Street, Pawtucket, 726-2080) is an outlet store for bed, bath, and kitchen, with deeply discounted bed linens, pillows, comforters, and towels (sold by the pound).

SECRET
SHOPPING
✤

The Arcade (65 Weybosset Street, 272-2340), built in 1828, is the oldest indoor marketplace in the United States. The two owners agreed on everything but what the facades should look like. In the fine Rhode Island spirit, instead of reaching a compromise that neither of them really liked, they each hired an architect for one end, and these architects designed facades to please each. So be sure to go through the building and compare the different ends. Inside, three stepped-back tiers are bordered by the original iron railings. First-floor food courts sell everything from ice cream to egg rolls. Upper-floor boutiques and shops show clothing, accessories, crafts, and antiques. It's especially lively at lunch.

SECRET SMOKE-FREE GREASY SPOON

❦

Loui's (286 Brook Street, 861-5225) is an institution. Started by two buddies after they got out of the Forces in 1945, this lunch-counter restaurant dishes up the usual fare, plus some unexpected bonuses — you can try out a number of vegetarian options that go beyond meat dishes minus the meat. It is noisy, crowded with Brown and RISD students, and worn from constant use — the tribute of generations of undergrad adulation. The paper cups feature a sketch of the veteran founders, arms over one another's necks, in uniform. And the smoke-free status — a big step for a college hangout in the diner mode — came about because Loui's beloved wife was diagnosed with serious lung disease many years ago. She continued to sit behind the register as she always had, reigning with confidence from her perch on a stool — but with an oxygen tank beside her — until she succumbed to death by tobacco a few years back. Loui's is still smoke free, which is pretty darn cool for a diner lover like me, since I'm allergic to tobacco.

SECRET SMOKING SECTION

❦

Wickenden Street is home to two smoking-related establishments. **Ethnic Concepts** (335 Wickenden Street, 454-7473) is rather transparent in one of its purposes. Along with posters for Hendrix, American Spirit cigs, and grateful dancing bear Beanie Babies, it advertises rolling papers and water pipes — for use with tobacco only, of course. The other purpose, though, is more cryptic. They sell used records in half the shop, and the other half looks like the living room of a 30-year-old guy who works in a record shop and has great plans for his life once he can pry himself away from the TV. And there my imagined guy sits, with a bunch of other guys, smoking cigars, watching TV, or talking about any old thing. The furniture is mismatched, the atmosphere is clearly that of a bunch of friends hanging out, and I have no idea what it's about because I'm too shy to ask and I'm allergic to nicotine. I give you this knowledge, so that if you are bolder than I, and if you enjoy cigars, you can perhaps make use of this curious and fascinating club.

Less secret is **Cafe Paragon** (234 Thayer Street, 331-6200), but it's for a really different smoking crowd. Euro-guys with outrageously overpriced cigars are encouraged to smoke to their hearts' content in the bar, coddled in leather chairs. Waitresses are carefully selected for appearances and style — to be a Paragon Girl has a certain cachet in the right circles. Circles that apparently value a permanent aroma of cigar smoke in women's hair.

SECRET SNAILS
❦

A friend and old roommate of mine turned me on to a Rhode Island delicacy, scungili — a title that lets you mentally gloss over the notion that you are ordering snail salad. My friend, in fact, might be the world expert on the dish, as he wrote his senior thesis on snail salad as a Folklore and Mythology concentrator at Harvard. Scungili is not very common at all, and I know of only a couple of diners that still serve this Italian treat the way it was meant to be. **Prairie Diner** (416 Public Street, 785-1658) carries it most of the time and I've heard that **Seaplane Diner** (307 Allen's Avenue, 941-9547) does too, though I haven't had it there myself.

SECRET SOUP

Spoons (485 Angell Street, 272-7687) is so unfancy that it looks as though they opened before they finished remodeling. It's not so much an eat-in place, though certainly you can, as it is a place to swing past to grab dinner on your way home. Seasonally changing soups are sold in pint or quart containers, and if you are a good cook, you could pass them off as homemade. They give you a piece of bread with each pint you buy. Now isn't that sweet? Flavors are wide ranging, from classics like beef barley to newfangled butternut squash, and there's always a vegetarian one. The containers could go into the freezer as easily as the microwave, forestalling the need to swing by too often. The restaurant was opened by an area chef whose soups were so popular he had people trying to get take-out. I, for one, am pleased he chose to keep his integrity and soups intact, by selling them fresh instead of canned.

SECRET
STROLL

✤

Sometimes, it's the most obvious we overlook the longest. A four-acre public park bordering the Providence River in the center of the city, **Waterplace Park** is a clean, well-lighted place for nighttime strolling. Its walls are made from the granite blocks of a former railroad abutment and informative panels describe and show the history of the area. A pond, a fountain, benches, lawns, and walking and bicycling paths make up the park, and an amphitheater provides a place for concerts and performances.

SECRET
SUBTERRANEAN DUCKPINS

✤

If you need to be told what duckpins are, you probably won't travel out to **Down Under Duckpin Bowling** (615 Pawtucket Avenue, Pawtucket, 725-1077), let alone enter the tiny cement building that's the only part of the business that shows above ground. Down under indeed, beneath a parking lot, these hidden lanes hide a sport that knows no age barriers. It's almost heartening to know that there's something people don't have to be over 35 to mourn the near demise of. The last duckpin lane may have closed in Baltimore, but Providence still has at least two others that we know of: **Dudek Bowling Alleys**

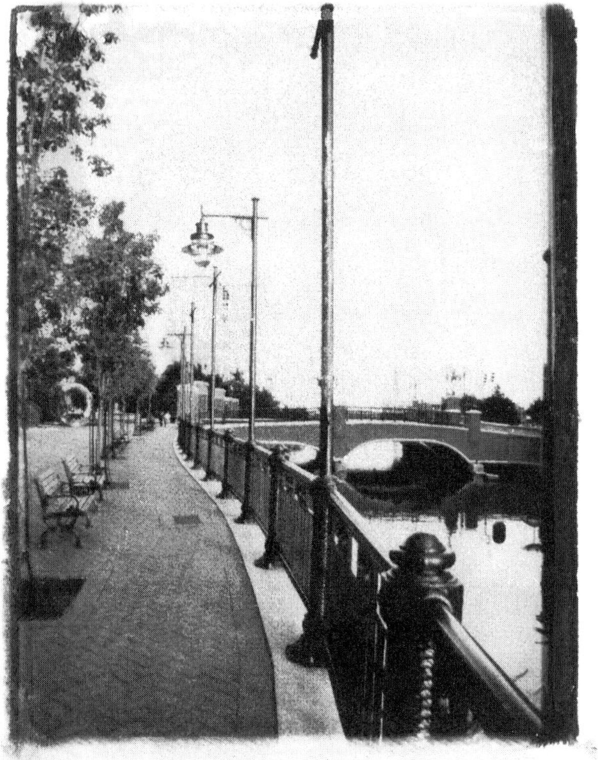

(417 Child Street, Warren, 245-9471) and **Bowling Academy, Inc.** (354 Taunton Avenue, East Providence, 434-5839).

SECRET
SUKIYAKI
❖

Far from the bustle of Wickenden Street's sushi purveyors, down on Hope Street just before it enters Pawtucket, is the new but winning **Ran Zan** (1084 Hope Street, 276-7574). Sharing a block with Maximillian's Ice Cream (see "Secret Ice Cream"), the modestly sized restaurant serves a world of Japanese foods beyond sushi. The appetizers are a Greatest Hits of Japanese Bar Food — yakitori, fresh tofu, spinach salad, gyoza, pickles, edamame... only the ginger-marinated chicken left me pining for better in *izakaya* I had known (*izakaya* are Japanese tapas bars, in essence — beer, sake, and munchies). Entrees are the Japanese standards, well prepared and flavorful. The sushi bar is, as usual, in full sight of the rest of the room, and if conversation hits a lull it makes good entertainment. Fish is fresh, nicely prepared, and properly seasoned. Wait staff is unassuming, a little overwhelmed, and very nice.

SECRET
SWEET TOOTH
❖

Federal Hill, the bastion of Italian-ness, has two pastry shops I recommend for very different purposes. **Scialo Bros. Bakery**

(257 Atwells Avenue, 421-0986) decorates the neighborhood's main street with the most stunning mid-20th-century facade and interior I have ever seen, in polished black stone, bakery name blazoned proudly. The windows onto the street are immaculately tiled, slightly slanted toward the sidewalk so you can get a good look at the sample wedding cake and other eye-catching goodies displayed to striking advantage. The interior is just as well kept as it must have been the day it opened — glass counters run up both sides and around the back, housing pastries, cakes, cookies, and candies safe from fingers and salivating customers until they are whisked away to be boxed up. Shelves behind the counters are stocked with more goods, mirrors add brightness, and the whole place just makes me feel like I should be bumping into Cary Grant any minute. And me without my hat and gloves.

The other spot is **Pastiche** (92 Spruce Street, 861-5190), on a side street parallel to Atwells Avenue. Pastiche is a pastry shop in a modern romantic mode, with a fondness for France clearly inspiring the pastry chef to create jewel-like fruit tarts; rich, dark chocolate gateaux; and multi-level tortes full of nuts, butter, and cream. Many restaurants in town without their own pastry chef advertise they get their desserts from Pastiche, and you know you've really got friends if a Pastiche box shows up at your surprise birthday party. The shop has a few tables, for which there is usually a line come evening. That makes it a little less romantic for a date with some cutie with a sweet tooth. The bustle does give that welcoming little shop front, busting with sugar and light, a glamour of its own.

SECRET
SWORDS AND SOLDIERS
❧

One of the reasons I hope Brown doesn't combine all its collections into one boring art-dominated museum is that I fear it will spell doom for all the wonderful special collections that are now visible. In a shiny new museum, they might all be stored away, and you'd have to make an appointment and show academic need to be able to see them. Hopefully, those who bequeathed some of these collections foresaw this sort of latter-day folly and made appropriate stipulations in their bequests. Now I'll hop down from my soapbox and get to the point: the charming and historically fascinating collection of toy soldiers in the **John Hay Library** (20 Prospect Street, 863-2414). Most of the 5,000-plus miniature soldiers are in full sets representing a particular regiment (mostly British) or campaign. But others show ceremonial scenes, such as coronations, and royal processions, such as one of King George V in his gold-covered coach, escorted by the Yeomen of the Guard and Life Guards. Others depict scenes from the Raj, the Foreign Legion, kilted Gordon Highlanders, or the 24th Foot Regiment in battle with the Zulus. Lead camels and their riders, elephants bearing hoodahs, miniature artillery, even the Swedish royal barge, are all displayed at eye level. Easy to miss, but for the faded lettering of its attached label, is a set of wooden soldiers used by Napoleon to plan his strategy. Ask at the main desk to see the collection, which is open to the public but in a special gallery upstairs.

The sword collection was left to Brown by the same woman, whose fascination with military uniforms led her to amass one of the world's finest collections of military items. Displayed at the **Annmary Brown Memorial** (21 Brown Street, 863-1994), the collection contains some very rare blades, including those of regiments that existed for only a short time.

SECRET TEA PARTIES
✣

Boston's Tea Party is well known, but in 1775, rebellious Providence residents burned tea at the **Market House**, beside the river on South Main Street. You'll see a plaque on the corner of the building commemorating this early manifestation of Rhode Island's politically incorrect behavior.

For a more modern tea party, walk around the corner to **L'Elizabeth** (285 South Main Street, 864-1974), a genteel and stylish cafe where you can sink into a cushy armchair and sip your tea from a fine china cup. Appropriate pastries accompany your tea, or you can have espresso and a late dessert here after the theater.

SECRET THAI
✣

A cave-like tunnel welcomes you incongruously to **Pakarang** (303 South Main Street, 453-3660), possibly left over from a '60s nightspot named something like "The Cave." But if that makes you wonder whether you've really found the Thai restaurant you sought, stepping out into the recycled sushi bar may confuse you even farther. But whatever used to be there before, it's resoundingly Thai now. Nearly 50 entree choices may include wild boar basil and will certainly include several shrimp choices.

SECRET
THEATERS RESTORED

The **Providence Performing Arts Center** (220 Weybosset Street, 421-ARTS, www.ppacri.org) occupies the 1928 Loews State Theater, which has been completely restored and now gleams in its original Beaux Arts grandeur. It's still a theater, with full Broadway stage productions, opera, and top international performers, as well as a big movie screen.

South of Providence, in the affluent little town of East Greenwich, the classic interior of the **Greenwich Odeum** (11 Main Street, East Greenwich, 885-9119, www.greenwichodeum.com) has been restored. Restored too is the theater's position in the community as a center for the performing arts. The Odeum is the venue for touring companies performing drama, opera, jazz, symphonic music, and dance, such as the National Shakespeare Company. Tickets to all performances are available at the East Village Greenwich Chamber of Commerce (591 Main Street, 885-0020).

110 SECRET PROVIDENCE

SECRET
TIME TO STAY AWAY
✢

The last weekend of May is Brown commencement. It's a good time to avoid Providence, since every available hotel room, restaurant, and parking space is filled. Earlier in the month are the graduations of Providence College and Rhode Island College, making May the tightest month in which to find lodging.

SECRET
TRAILS
✢

A major state park surrounding Olney Pond, its proximity to the city makes **Lincoln Woods State Park** (Eddie Dowling Highway [Route 146], Lincoln, 723-7892) very popular and busy in the middle of the summer. In spring or fall it's a different place, quiet and empty, where you can walk in solitude along several paved roads or woodland trails. Trail maps are free.

Blackstone River Valley National Heritage Corridor (1 Depot Square, Woonsocket, 762-0440) is a linear park that follows the Blackstone Canal. The former towpath is the best place to see the remains of the canal and to get a sense of how it operated. Some sections of the canal are so well preserved that they look as though they could re-open tomorrow; others are barely discernable.

SECRET
TRANSPORT
❖

In an effort to make it easy for people to get to their new Providence Place Mall, its promoters have provided a free shuttle bus that connects Downcity, the colleges, and other parts of town with the mall, which is close to Waterplace Park.

The city's public transport is provided by the Rhode Island Public Transit Authority (RIPTA), the excellent state-wide transit system. The in-city fare is 50 cents. Pick up a bus plan and schedules at the bus terminal on Kennedy Plaza. RIPTA buses also connect Providence to T.F. Green Airport, a 15-minute trip, at least hourly. The fare is $1.40 from Kennedy Plaza to the airport, which sure beats the $20-plus taxi fare. For cheap water ferries to both Newport and Pawtucket, see "Secret Cruises."

SECRET
TREASURE TROVES
❖

The Rhode Island School of Design Museum (224 Benefit Street, 454-6500, www.risd.edu) defies classification. It is essentially an art museum and is certainly the state's foremost one. But, like most great art museums, it is filled with treasures that go far beyond art — Egyptian mummies, the serenely beautiful wooden Heian Buddha, an outstanding collection of 18th-century furniture, Roman marbles, Peruvian burial cloths. What I enjoy most about the RISD Museum is that, instead of arranging art and artifacts by culture, it displays them chronologically. This unusual juxtaposition of contemporary pieces from far distant cultures gives visitors a fascinating new perspective.

While it may not have mummies, **Tilden-Thurber Co.** (292 Westminster Street, 272-3200) is a museum in its own right. Although its art works and antiquities equal those of many museums, everything here is for sale. Leave your credit cards at home before going to browse in one of the nation's finest collections of American furniture from the neo-Classical (post-Colonial) period.

SECRET VEGETARIAN

The world needs more veggie restaurants like **Garden Grille** (727 East Avenue, Pawtucket, 726-2826). This is right at the city line, just off Hope Street at the corner of Lafayette Street. It makes amazingly flavorful, filling, energizing food that coincidentally doesn't have any meat in it. I know it's no accident to the Garden Grille, but too depressingly often, vegetarian menu options are like a friend with amnesia — they are there, but something intrinsic is missing. Like a veggie BLT. Tofu just can't be bacon.

Garden Grille has gotten over the notion that people who want to eat veggie want to eat facsimiles of meat. They do have soy-based proteins in their foods, but not in a contrived way. They cook a mean legume, though, and for that I applaud them. After a hot chickpea curry wrap I had there, I felt like I could wrestle Godzilla, it was so full of virtuous stuff and flavor. While smoothies and wraps are the

SECRET PROVIDENCE

bulk of the menu, these go far past those served at the kind of joint you see in every college town.

SECRET
VENICE
✤

You've read about **La Gondola** (Citizen's Bank Plaza, 421-8877; in Boston, 508-984-8264) in the *New York Times* and the *Wall Street Journal*, and seen it in the TV series "Providence," and I'm going to pass it off as a secret? Of course not. But one secret is that you can reserve it during WaterFire. You just need to call waaaay in advance. The other secret is that, while the usual 40-minute trip costs $60 for two (and extra for up to six), for as little as $10 each, three people can have a 20-minute ride. You can't reserve these short rides, but if one of the gondolas is sitting idle, it's probably available at these walk-up rates. The original Providence gondola is believed to be the first authentic gondola ever constructed in the US; the second one was built in Venice. Each has more than 250 feet of solid brass trim. They're handsome craft, and a ride under the arched brick bridges is pure romantic fun.

SECRET
VICTORIAN
✤

You'll notice the **Governor Henry Lippitt House** (199 Hope Street, 453-0688) as you drive or walk past, due to its size and its

SECRET PROVIDENCE

beautiful condition. But you would never guess at the interior it hides. Decorated with stenciled ceilings, stained and etched glass, faux marble, and false grained woods, it is among New England's finest interiors and perhaps the very best in Victorian decorative styles.

You can stay overnight in a fine Victorian house, **The Old Court** (144 Benefit Street, 751-2002). This Italianate mansion on Benefit Street's Mile of History has become an inn, and its high-ceilinged rooms, most with beautiful architectural details, are decorated with fine antiques and carpets. Two of the rooms have televisions, all have air conditioning, and the inn has a washer and dryer for guests to use. Not authentic to the period, of course, but very convenient.

SECRET VIEWS

Atop College Hill, **Prospect Park** (Congdon Street, at Cushing Street, see "Secret Pranks") is the burial place of Roger Williams. His statue gazes out over one of the best views of the city he founded. The land drops sharply away, revealing a vista of the entire downtown area. Climb the hill on Meeting Street, then turn left onto Congdon.

My favorite perspective on Waterplace Park and the river is from the glass elevator at the **Providence Biltmore** (Kennedy Plaza, 421-0700 or 1-800-294-7709, www.providencebiltmore.com). The Biltmore gleams with turn-of-the-century elegance. A walk through its grand lobby always makes me feel good — especially when I think of how close this building came, like the City Hall beside it, to falling under a wrecking ball. I'm glad it's still here.

SECRET VINEYARDS

Diamond Hill Vineyards (3145 Diamond Hill Road [Route 114], Cumberland, 333-2751 or 1-800-752-2505) began a quarter century ago, when the first vines were planted. Now more than five acres are planted with pinot noir grapes and 15 acres are given over to fruit orchards. Inside the 200-year-old farmhouse are the gift shop and tasting rooms, where you can sample the pinot noir and wines made from apples, peaches, plums, and blueberries. From April through November, vineyard tours are given hourly on the half hour.

SECRET WEDDING RECEPTIONS

For an elegant reception, you can reserve the former **Roger Williams Park Casino** (785-9450). This elegant pavilion's large windows overlook the lake, and its porticoes are surrounded by flowerbeds in the summer. The interior woodwork is hand finished to a warm patina and the original maple floors are still intact.

SECRET WEEKNIGHT DEAL

Restaurants don't get much smaller and more intimate than **New Rivers** (7 Steeple Street, 751-0350). A varied, seasonal, and sophisticated menu almost constantly surprises me, sometimes pairing fruits with meat, often substituting unexpected vegetables in old favorite dishes. Presentation is stylish, and always appropriate to the dish. The wine list is particularly good, both in selection and price. And the deal is a three-course *prix fixe* in the middle of the week (Tuesday through Thursday) at the usual price of an entree alone.

SECRET WIENERS

Nowhere in New York have I ever seen anything like what are known here as New York System Wieners. Only in Rhode Island can you find steamed hot dogs smothered in quickly blanched chopped onion — and each purveyor's secret blend of seasonings. My favorite place remains **Olneyville New York System** (20 Plainville Street, Olneyville, 621-9500). The price is right, the dogs are good, and it's a slice of local culture that would make the heart of any anthropologist beat faster.

SECRET PROVIDENCE

SECRET WILDFLOWERS
✤

Lime Rock Preserve (Wilbur Road, off Route 123, Lincoln, 331-7110) is a 157-acre property of the Nature Conservancy near Lime Rock, north of Providence. The marble outcrops around the pond give the first clue that the soil here differs from the predominantly acid soil of the rest of the state. On a moderate two-mile walk along the bed of the old Providence/Woonsocket trolley line, you may see northern green orchids, yellow lady slippers, fringed gentians, and several varieties of bloodroot. There are also ferns, both on the rocks and on the forest floor.

SECRET WINTER LIFT
✤

No matter what the weather outside, it's always summer inside the **Charles H. Smith Greenhouse** (Roger Williams Park, 785-9450). Several greenhouses are filled with bloom all year, and are open daily (free). The flower displays include an excellent collection of orchids. In November, the Annual Chrysanthemum Show fills the greenhouses with masses of this symbol of autumn, in colors and sizes you never dreamed possible. In December, an extravaganza of brilliant poinsettias is on display during the two middle weeks of the month. In the summer, the outdoor beds that surround the greenhouses are filled with solid color.

SECRET
WISE WOMEN

It can be alarmingly difficult to find non-culinary herbs in many cities. I lived for years having to save my herb shopping for visits to my old hometown, until **Indigo Herbals** (346 Wickenden Street, 274-6939, www.indigoherbals.com) opened and I could finally buy ingredients for my favorite herbal tea and bath sachets close to home. It's a beautiful, otherworldly little shop, painted a lovely lavender blue, with a medieval lady gracing the back wall.

Herbs are sold in bulk by weight, and you can buy as much or as little as you need, at very reasonable prices. The shop also carries oils and other ingredients you need to make your own herbal remedies, lotions, balms, and toiletries. When I needed aloe vera gel and pure lanolin, I knew Indigo Herbals would have them. The proprietress apprenticed with another herbalist in Rhode Island for some time before she opened her shop in 1999. She is very knowledgeable about herbs' properties and applications, and is a fountain of information on alternative health care options in the area. The shop stocks a carefully chosen selection of books on herbal and natural remedies, alternative health care, and Wicca with a women's focus, plus flower and herb remedies, and a great selection of toiletries, some of which are locally made.

SECRET
NEWPORT

SECRET ABLUTIONS

Remember how they always said you had to kiss a lot of frogs to find the handsome prince? It's like that looking for the great tubs and showers — you can bet we're squeaky clean after researching this one. The best secret shower is at **Cliffside Inn** (2 Seaview Avenue, 847-1811 or 1-800-845-1811), in the Governor's Room. It's a genuine Victorian birdcage shower, 120 years old. At the same inn, Beatrice's Room has a tub set into the bay window. For some of the inn's other secrets, see "Secret Artist."

For a less fancy, but clean, place to wash off the salt water when you hit town by boat, Newport's only public showers — for which you pay a modest $2 on the honor system — are at the **Seaman's Church Institute** (Market Square, at America's Cup Avenue, 847-4260). This mission was designed for arriving sailors and still serves that purpose under the sponsorship of the Episcopal Church. You can also ablut your laundry in the institute's washers and dryers.

SECRET ACCESS

While you might not expect that a city whose main attractions are historic properties would be readily accessible to wheelchairs, Newport is surprisingly so. For addresses and telephone numbers of the attractions listed below, see their individual listings.

Most of the mansions were built after the elevator was invented, and their owners could afford all the modern conveniences. **Belcourt Castle**, **The Breakers**, and **The Elms** have elevators to reach upper floors, although the width of the elevator at The Elms may not accommodate some wheelchairs, and the mansion's Behind the Scenes tour goes into areas with very limited access. Proprietors of the mansions ask visitors to call about access before visiting.

The **Naval War College Museum** and the **Newport Yachting Center** have wheelchair access, as do the **Newport Art Museum** and **Green Animals**, although the latter two's restrooms do not. The same is true of the **Block Island Ferry**: the boat itself is accessible, but its restrooms are not.

The city's most historic lodging, the **Francis Malbone House**, has a specially designed room with wheelchair access. Chain hotels and most restaurants can accommodate wheelchairs. Most churches, including **Trinity Church**, are also accessible.

The Newport Convention and Visitors Bureau will send you a list of accessible lodgings, shops, restaurants, and attractions (849-8048 or 1-800-326-6030). The visitors' center itself is fully accessible.

SECRET
AERIE
✤

In the middle of Narragansett Bay, off Newport, the **Rose Island Lighthouse** (847-4242) sweeps the harbor and bay each night with its bright beam. But during the day, it's the best perch in Newport. Sitting in this small lantern room, surrounded by glass and far above the water, you have a 360-degree view of the town, its harbor, the shipping channel, the Newport Bridge, and the Jamestown shore as far as Fort Wetherill. You can watch the steady flow of boats and ships, from sailing yachts and lobstermen to Navy ships and freighters from all over the world. And it's just you and the birds.

You can visit the 1870 lighthouse and climb to its lantern room as part of a regular tour that leaves from Ann Street Wharf, but if you want this tower room as your own private aerie, you have to sign on as lighthouse keeper for a week. It's not very expensive, and along with use of the attractive, modern upstairs apartment, you get to make the official weather observations and keep the lighthouse running smoothly. It takes a couple of hours' work each day. The rest of the time, you can listen in on boat chatter and the Coast Guard on the marine band radio, or just sit in your solitary tower and watch the ships go by.

SECRET
AL FRESCO

Despite Newport's dependable sea breeze, summer evenings are usually warm, and dining outdoors is a good way to enjoy them. Of course, you can join the throngs at the wharf-side pubs and eateries, but I like a more secluded place to dine *al fresco*. I found it at **La Petite Auberge** (19 Charles Street, 849-6669). Behind the intimate and beautifully appointed dining rooms of this tiny historic house is an enclosed courtyard, where the atmosphere is a bit less formal, but the service, menu, and extraordinary French wine list are the same.

Whatever you order from the list of French classics, and however high your cholesterol level, don't bypass (sorry, inappropriate choice of verb there) the pâté.

SECRET AMBROSIA

Socialite John Drexel recalls whiling away afternoons by slipping into a state of euphoria as his hostess plied him with the Gilded Age's favorite afternoon cocktail, a **White Lady**. The secret "recipe" (everyone had his own proportions) is orange liqueur, lemon juice, egg whites for froth, and "lots of gin."

SECRET AMERICA'S CUP

If you follow yacht racing, you'll have seen what is possibly the most famous photograph in yachting history. It was taken in 1983, when they dropped the curtain and the world saw for the first time the winged keel. You can stand on the spot where the picture was taken, on Bowen's Wharf, where the small hut housing the hoist motor is clearly visible in the water. Stand there, close your eyes, and you can almost hear the gasp as the curtain dropped. It was one of the most electrifying moments in Newport history. Until then, everybody knew what a keel looked like — it looked like a keel. How, they wondered, could *Australia II* have gotten this far, looking so different, without anyone getting wind of it? This is where the world first saw underneath the boat that was to change racing history with its revolutionary new aquadynamic.

Herreshoff Manufacturing Company, which built eight America's Cup winners, and the cream of racing and cruising yachts, closed in 1945 after more than 80 years of fine boat building. At its boatyards you'll now find the **Herreshoff Marine Museum** (7 Burnside Street, Bristol, 253-5000, herreshoff@ids.net). Spotlighting the sleekest and fastest yachts of their time, as well as their design and construction, the heart of the collections is the Hall of Boats, where you can see more than 45 examples of the genius of their designers. From *Sprite*, which Nathanael Herreshoff called "the first of what became my life's work" (he was 11 years old when he made the drawings for it), to the *Defiance*, you can see how yacht design changed without ever losing its beauty.

The **America's Cup Hall of Fame**, part of the same complex, honors sailors, yachtsmen, and designers, and includes a piece of the keel of the original *America*, along with half-hull models of all American America's Cup winners and many primary contenders. Kids can learn about boats in the hands-on Discovery Center.

SECRET ANCESTORS

֍

Lacking impressive lineages of their own, Newport's mansion owners struggled hard to be part of European aristocracy, marrying their

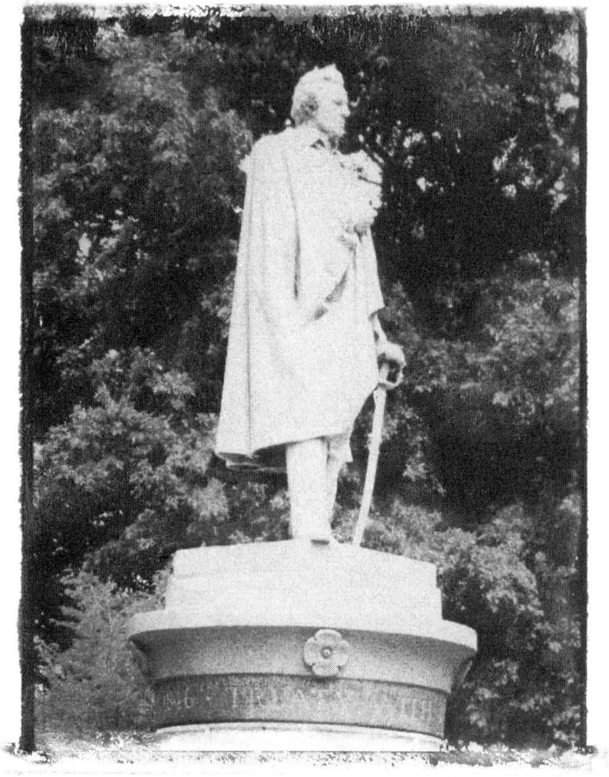

daughters (often unwillingly) to British nobles by providing handsome dowries. This need for an aristocratic family tree prompted them to hang their summer palaces with royal portraits. Even though these didn't picture their own forebears, the *nouveaux riches* could feel more connected by passing daily under a royal gaze.

But for the rest of us, especially those whose real ancestors were involved in the China or Triangle Trade (either as seamen or as human cargo), and for those tracing early American Jewish or Quaker families, Newport offers some excellent resources.

The **Newport Historical Society** (82 Touro Street, 846-0813) has the complete records of America's oldest Quaker congregation, the account books and records of Aaron Lopez and other early Jewish merchants, account books of the slave traders, ships' logs of many sailing ships based in Newport, and the second-largest genealogical library in Rhode Island. It also has an extensive local history library, collections of decorative arts, and Newport silver and furniture.

SECRET ANIMALS

Always trying to out-do one another, Newport's summer set doted on exotic pets. Doris Duke kept a pair of camels at Rough Point. They reposed in a canopy tent on the lawn, and stuck their heads into the glorious solarium to be fed graham crackers. In the hurricane of 1991, Princess and Baby were brought into the solarium for protection and broke part of the mirror to the right of the door.

Exotic pets of a different sort were kept at **Green Animals** (Cory's Lane, off Route 114, Portsmouth, 847-1000), formerly the estate of the Brayton family. Their talented Portuguese gardener, Joseph Carreiro, created a topiary camel from living shrubs, modeling it after the one on a box of Dromedary dates. Close by, in the formal garden, he sculpted a topiary giraffe, a more ambitious and challenging task. In the 1938 hurricane, its neck was broken, and it has never quite regained its regal height.

Many other creatures romp nearby. These extraordinary gardens — they have only one or two peers in North America — are created in the European topiary tradition from boxwood and privet, but go far beyond the stylized spirals, balls, and arches of traditional topiary. Whimsical animals are the main feature, although the gardens they stand in are a work of art, too. Bears, dogs, and a unicorn, boar, reindeer, ostrich, swan, donkey, lion, and elephant keep the giraffe and camel company.

SECRET ANIME

⚜

Need a quick fix of *This is Greenwood*, *Urotsukidoji*, or *Neon Genesis Evangelion*? **The Annex** (314 Broadway, 847-4607) can provide it, along with Hong Kong and Samurai rentals. Comic books of all genres — current and back issues — join the video action, and The Annex is open every day.

SECRET
AROMAS
✥

Center yourself by just inhaling the air inside **Tea & Herb Essence** (476 Thames Street, 847-7423 or 1-800-988-4372, www.teaandherb.com). The aromatherapy begins as you walk in the door, and jars of herbs and fragrant blossoms, essential oils, herb and flower extracts, and a complete line of natural bath and body products provide everything you need for more prolonged pampering. Tea lovers come here for the good selection of bulk teas: green, black, and herbal.

SECRET
ART
✥

Although the main claim to fame of the **Redwood Library and Athenaeum** (50 Bellevue Avenue, 847-0292) is that it's the oldest library building in America (it was begun in 1748), it also houses some very fine artworks. Here you can see three of Gilbert Stuart's earliest works, completed when he was only a teenager. He did them before receiving formal training, so he hid the hands of his subjects. They're quite a long way from the later works of the man who was the "official" portrait painter of the founding fathers. The portrait of George Washington is a copy done by Stuart's very talented daughter, Jane. Also in the library are New England's oldest known Windsor chairs, other paintings, and changing exhibits of art and illustrated manuscripts. Books are loaned only to members, but you can use them there, and the collections of paintings and decorative arts are on view without an admission charge, Monday through Saturday.

If you collect "firsts," the Redwood has more: it is the first neo-classical building in America, and the first work of America's first architect, Peter Harrison, a merchant sea captain who began designing as an amateur. He went on to do Newport's Touro Synagogue and King's Chapel in Boston.

SECRET ARTILLERY
※

Here we go with the Newport superlatives again, but the **Artillery Company of Newport** (23 Clarke Street, 846-8488) is the oldest continuously active company in the US. Founded in 1741 under a charter from King George II, it's older than the country itself. On display in the 1835 armory are uniforms, weapons, and military items from all seven wars the company took part in, including the flag flown by Oliver Hazard Perry at the Battle of Lake Erie.

SECRET ARTIST
※

Few artists present quite the enigma that the reclusive and talented Beatrice Turner does. Very few originals of her work are known to remain, all of them portraits and almost all of them of herself. To say that she was eccentric doesn't begin to tell the story. Her father took her out of art school when he learned that they used live models, and from then on she had no model other than herself — and occasionally her mother. That doesn't seem to have turned her against her father, with whom she had such a close — and, some suggest, unnatural — relationship that when he died, she painted the huge Victorian house black. As you can imagine, the neighbors were not pleased.

The house has long since been repainted, and more recently restored as the charming **Cliffside Inn** (2 Seaview Avenue, 847-1811 or 1-800-845-1811). Although the paintings that once covered the walls were burned as worthless by later owners, reproductions from photographs hang throughout the public rooms. The owners have made it their mission to identify other Beatrice Turner paintings that may still exist. They will certainly tell you the story of the people who stayed here and later recognized a Turner painting at a flea market.

Rooms are bright and airy, many overlooking the water through the tall trees that surround its hillside setting. All but two rooms have whirlpool baths, and each has its own individual style. The Blue Room, for example has a sunny window seat, and the Victorian Room on the first floor has a cameo sofa. I, personally, retreat to the solitary splendor of the vertical Tower Suite, with its own wonderfully discreet private entrance, bay window seat, and posh bathroom that occupies the entire first floor. Throughout the inn, television sets are well hidden behind paintings, and most guests leave them there, preferring a restful, quiet stay.

SECRET
ASTRAL BODIES

If you were a ghost, what better place to choose than a great pile of gray stones filled with medieval accoutrements? So many ghostly sightings have been reported at **Belcourt Castle** (659 Bellevue Avenue, 846-0669) that they're almost commonplace, and a lot of them center on a single chair. The incident with the most witnesses occurred during one of the mansion's regular Ghost Tours, when the guide was pointing out the chair. As she explained that many people report a tingling feeling when they hold their hand over it, a woman on the tour sat down in the chair and was promptly thrown out. When she sat down again, she was once more unceremoniously catapulted from the chair, as though a spring had released. The family who owns and lives in the castle has other stories of their experiences, including tales of a screaming suit of armor and several appearances of a monk.

The setting is certainly right. This castle took more than 300 European stonemasons, woodcarvers, and other artists four years to build, and it could pass for at least a couple of centuries older than it is, with its great hall, dark paneling, and windows of genuine 13th-century stained glass (America's best assemblage, by the way). Unlike the other major mansions, you don't have to take a tour here but can explore it alone, reading the signs and labels. Or you can join a tour, where you will learn some of the house's history. Belcourt is known especially for its collection of armor, as good a resting place for astral bodies as I can think of. The place is a rich museum of art and antiquities, with trinkets from Versailles, the Tuilleries, the Imperial Palace in Peking, and the temple of Amenhotep.

Theme tours of Belcourt, usually on Thursdays, focus on ghosts. They are always the most popular tours during **Haunted Newport** (849-8048 or 1-800-326-6030, www.hauntednewport.com), a series of events that spans October and zeroes in on unexplained phenomena and ghostly good times.

Belcourt Castle is not the only place in Newport with ghost stories. According to *Haunted Newport*, a lively little book by Eleyne Austen Sharp (Open Mind, www.austensharp.com), several former mansions-turned-dorms at Salve Regina University have strange doings (other than the usual strange doings in college dorms, that is).

The ghost of Stephen Decatur — or another dressed in a similar uniform — is said to haunt his birthplace on Charles Street, now **La Petite Auberge** (19 Charles Street, 849-6669, see "Secret Al Fresco").

Such historic buildings seem to attract astral bodies, especially those with an eventful past. The **White Horse Tavern** (26 Marlborough Street, at Farewell Avenue, 849-3600) is the oldest operating tavern in the United States, opening prior to 1673. Local lore holds that the site of Colony House, once Rhode Island's capitol, was chosen so it would be an easy distance from the tavern. Along with its ghosts — which employees have reported seeing and hearing in the late hours of the evening — it offers an authentic colonial tavern setting and a menu of old-fashioned favorites (beef Wellington and rack of lamb), updated nicely with New American accompaniments. The decor is largely original, with very dark wood walls lit only by candlelight, so any spirits returning from their old tavern days would feel at home. Hopefully they'll dress properly for dinner, as you should, too, if you dine there.

The tavern's curator, Anita Raphael of **Newport on Foot** (846-5391, see "Secret Tours"), hosts tavern talks there on Friday mornings in the summer, as well as a walking tour of graveyards and ghostly sites in Newport. The ghost tour is offered only in October.

SECRET
AWFUL-AWFUL

If you're from Rhode Island, skip this — you already know it. But for the rest of you, an Awful-Awful is a thick, scrumptious ice cream drink created about 60 years ago by **Newport Creamery** (49 Long Wharf, 849-8469), before it had 40-some locations throughout the state. (You can tell how addictive the Awful-Awful is by their proliferation.) The Creamery, wherever you find one, is also a dependable place to get fish & chips or a burger. And if you can drink three Awful-Awfuls, they'll give you the fourth one free. Don't try it.

SECRET
B & B

You do have to bring your own breakfast — and cook it on a 1940s-vintage gas stove — but this is only one of the things that makes this B&B like no other. Take the location, for example. You can't just drive up to it and check in. You toss your suitcase and picnic basket onto a launch that takes you there. The "B&B" at **Rose Island Lighthouse** (847-4242) occupies the first floor of the old keeper's cottage, built into the tower itself. Unlike the modern second-floor keeper's apartment (see "Secret Aerie"), this one is restored to the way it looked in the 1940s, when a keeper and his family lived here full time.

During the day, you might have a small group of visitors come to see the island, and your house, but that's part of the fun. When they leave, the old player piano and the comfy rocker — and the rest of the island — are all yours, except for the apartment of the lighthouse keeper upstairs, who has radio contact with the mainland in case of emergency. But by their nature, keepers keep to themselves, or they wouldn't be there. You both have access to the tower's lantern room.

No electricity, no TV, no resort luxuries, no dozens of lace-covered pillows to remove before you climb under the genuine vintage patchwork quilt. I like it best in the winter, especially in a storm, when the wind howls and whistles and shakes the windowpanes, but the woodstove in the kitchen keeps the cottage cozy and you don't need to worry about the electricity going off. The wind can blow and the gas lamps keep going. Pack a basket of food (see "Secret Picnics") and a bottle of good wine. My S.O. and I spent Valentine's Day here once, and no place has matched it since.

SECRET
BACKSTAIRS
✣

A walk through Newport's mansions may leave you wondering how the servants moved about these houses. One can't exactly picture the maid with her mop and bucket descending the elegant staircase into the great hall of The Breakers. The answer is a complete set of passages and stairways used only by the staff, leading to kitchens, laundry rooms, pantries, closets, and servants' quarters, which were all known collectively as "backstairs." To reach a room, servants slid through small connecting doors, which were often seamlessly disguised and padded so these comings and goings were noiseless.

A tour of **Belcourt Castle** points out one of these doors in the library, so cleverly hidden that you would never notice it if someone didn't draw it to your attention.

A **Behind the Scenes at The Elms** tour (367 Bellevue Avenue, at Dixon Street, 847-1000) not only takes you through all these passageways and into the real workings of the building and the household, but its guide also provides a well-told and often amusing account of how things ran. The butler, the housekeeper, the chef, and the coachman were the main players. The butler commanded the footmen and the housekeeper ruled over all the maids and laundresses. She carried the keys to everything and counted each piece of linen as it left for the laundry and was returned to the linen closet. (A single piece of fine household linen could cost more than the annual salary of a top staff member.)

Edward Berwin, who built The Elms and lived in it for many years, took an interest in his summer home that was quite unlike the attitude of most other husbands of the Four Hundred. You'll see some of his inventions, such as a light bulb tester, as you tour the cavernous basements, with their laundry rooms, heating plant (coal burning, of course), food storage areas, wine cellars, and ice room. From the cellar, it's three flights up to the servants' quarters, which were roomier than most and a good deal nicer. In their midst is the giant cistern that provided water for the house. Four Behind the Scenes tours are given daily, and you should reserve, since spaces are limited.

SECRET BASEBALL

Few stadiums can replicate the feeling of old-time baseball like **Cardines Field** (America's Cup Avenue, at West Marlborough Street, 847-1398). Built during the Depression as a WPA project, it still provides a home for local Sunset League teams, which have been playing in Newport since 1919. Babe Ruth leagues play here, appropriately, because the Babe himself pitched exhibition games at Cardines when he was with the Boston Braves. The fans are noisy, the teams enthusiastic, and the games free. Part of the experience is to eat Newport's best fries next door at the **Mudville's Pub** (8 West Marlborough Street, 849-1408), which really deserves a place of its own under "Secret Fries." I don't know what they're fried in and don't want to, because it can't be good for me and taste that good.

SECRET BEACHES

Second Beach (see "Secret Surf") in Middletown is less crowded than Easton's Beach, but **Third Beach** has the most elbow room of these three large protected strands. Also, there is more likely to be parking space there. Some of the beach is private, so be careful to stay in the public areas. To get there from Memorial Boulevard, follow the shore into Middletown, turning right on Purgatory Road to the end, then Paradise Road to the left.

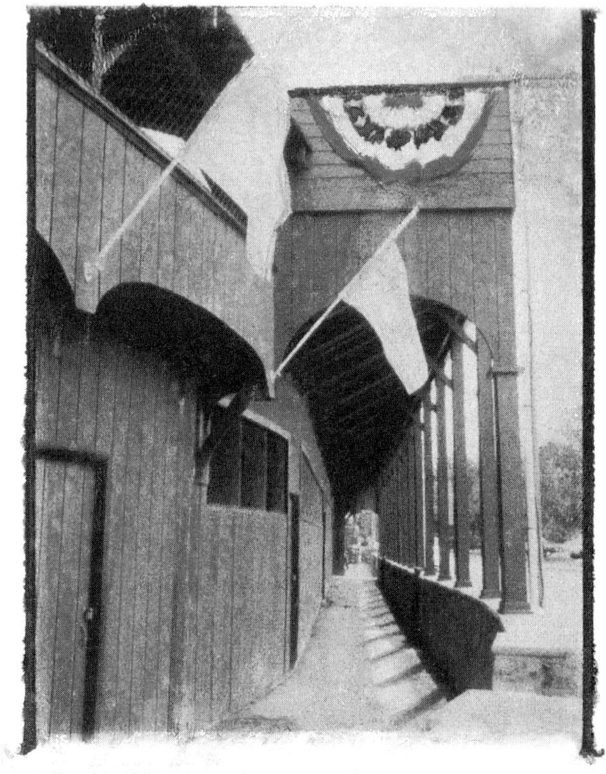

Island Park Beach and **Teddy's Beach** (at the Old Stone Bridge, Park Avenue off Route 138, Portsmouth) are both on the Sakonnet River north of Newport. Both are free, and they are close to each other, but Island Park has no lifeguard. Teddy's does, along with picnic tables.

Back in Newport, **Gooseberry Beach**, near (but not to be confused with, please) the very private Bailey's Beach, is a small strip of wavebeaten sand on Brenton Point Road.

SECRET
BIRDS
✤

The adjacent lands and coastlines of the **Norman Bird Sanctuary** (Third Beach Road, Middletown, 846-2577) and the **Sachuest National Wildlife Refuge** (Sachuest Point Road, Middletown, 364-9124) are alive with birds. This large and varied habitat is perfect for waterfowl and upland species — more than 250 species have been sighted — and is an important stopping place for migrating waterfowl and hawks. From the miles of walking trails, you might see merganser, bufflehead, and harlequin ducks, loons, grebes, and geese, along with shore birds such as sandpipers, piping plovers, great and snowy egrets, and great blue herons. Ospreys, hawks, and peregrine falcons stop here during migrations. A small natural history museum at the Norman Sanctuary illustrates the lifecycles of birds.

Conanicut Island Sanctuary (near the end of the Newport Bridge, Jamestown, 423-7220) adjoins a marsh where wading birds nest and several species of ducks winter. The entrance to the trail is opposite the Jamestown police station, where you can park. In winter, you can see songbird species that normally migrate south, in the bushes along the protected shore on the west side of **Beavertail State Park**.

Rose Island, in the middle of the bay, is a wading bird rookery for several species, mainly black-crowned night herons, glossy ibises, and great and snowy egrets. Before mid-June, you can't paddle closer than 20 yards from the shore to watch them.

SECRET BOOKSTORES

The Armchair Sailor (543 Thames Street, 847-4252) is for travelers, especially if they travel by water. Fill your duffel here with books on the sea, sailing, New England, maritime history, and general travel. While staff members are ready to help if there's a special book or subject you're pursuing, they will also leave you alone to browse in peace — and offer you a cup of tea while you do.

Just as friendly to browsers is **The Scribe's Perch Bookstore** (69-73 Long Wharf, 849-8426). Look here for out-of-print books on local history and New England history and traditions. Ask for a schedule of the store's lively rare-book auctions, well attended by book collectors and those who just love old volumes. The owner is quite an entertainment himself, as auctioneer.

The small shop at the **Newport Art Museum** (76 Bellevue Avenue, 848-8200) is a very good place to look for art books, especially on subjects that have some connection to Newport, its early craftsmen, the mansions and their collections, and local architecture. An even larger selection is available at the gift shop in the old staff dining room under the kitchens at **The Breakers** (Ochre Point Avenue, 847-1000).

SECRET
BREAD PUDDING
❦

For reasons I've never fathomed, Newporters crave bread pudding like the rest of the world craves chocolate. They compare notes on their favorite places to eat it, they order it even when there are far tastier (to me) things on the menu, and they would probably boycott a restaurant that stopped serving it. You'll always find it at the **White Horse Tavern** (see "Secret Astral Bodies"). When the Rumb Line closed, the local favorite for this homey little pud-made-good became **Le Bistro** (19 Bowen's Wharf, 849-7778), already popular for its sparkling French menu. It treats the bread pudding to a bourbon sauce. Even the ultimate bastion of Italy in Newport, **Puerini's** (see "Secret Veal"), serves bread pudding right alongside the caramel flan and the tiramisu.

SECRET
BREAKFASTS
❦

When news got out that **Franklin Spa** (229 Spring Street, 847-3540) was closing, a group of local people saved it. That's loyalty that only a serious neighborhood eatery could inspire. Breakfast is served throughout the restaurant's opening hours, from early morning until 3 PM (2 PM on Sunday), in a bright storefront setting. Hot muffins, good coffee, and fancier breakfast entrees, such as giant plates of fruit pancakes, are all on the menu. More stylish is **Cappuccino's** (92 Williams Street, off Bellevue Avenue, 846-7145), with white linens and a cute little patio where you can get French pastries and Sunday brunch dishes. Open longer hours, it doubles as a coffee shop, where you can find tortes and other pastries.

Our vote for the best breakfast in town goes to the **Adele Turner Inn** (93 Pelham Street, 847-1811 or 1-800-845-1811, www.adele turnerinn.com), beginning with the outstanding nutty granola, which you can heap with perfect fresh berries. (I was hoping to learn the recipe for the granola, but that's a secret that Donna — the gregarious hostess and chef — won't share. All she'll say is that it has half the oil and twice the nuts of standard granola, and is toasted a little longer.) A tiered tray of hot scones and muffins precedes a main course, when you may be offered a choice of omelettes, Belgian waffles, a "crepe cake" (crepes layered with fresh berries), or Greek egg cups (phyllo cases filled with olives, feta, mushrooms, and a poached egg, sauced with bearnaise). What makes these elegantly served breakfasts such a delight is that Donna is constantly re-inventing them.

Of course, you can't just wander in for breakfast, but staying there is a treat, too. All rooms are beautifully decorated in rich colors and fine fabrics, while still being comfortable. Some have whirlpool baths, and Room 11 has its own deck, with views of the harbor from Fort Adams to the Newport Bridge. Musicians love Room 2, with its violin, saxophone, and posters from past Newport festivals.

SECRET
CAMPING
⚜

Campgrounds are scarce in this neighborhood, which is why the town of Portsmouth took over former Navy land for the **Melville Pond Campground** (181 Bradford Road, off Route 114, Portsmouth, 849-8212) and the Melville Nature Preserve. Open sites with fire rings accommodate tents or RVs, and hot showers are available. Don't come expecting all the frills, like recreation centers and miniature golf, at this welcome addition to Newport's lodging options.

SECRET
CEILINGS
⚜

You're likely to leave town with a stiff neck from looking at all the knockout ceilings, each glittering with more gold than the last. Painted, vaulted, mullioned, frescoed, paneled — just about every type of decorated ceiling has been done here. But none is quite so exquisite — or has such a history — as that of the library at **Rosecliff** (Bellevue Avenue, 847-1000). Made entirely of plaster, its ornate and complicated design is formed by a series of 25 circles upon 25 circles on 25 clovers. From these hang inverted finials.

After Rosecliff and its furniture were sold at auction, no one thought to shut off the water for the winter (the housekeeper would never have forgotten that) and the pipes burst, soaking the elaborate ceiling. As the plaster absorbed the water, it disintegrated. When its new owners began the restoration after World War II, only one photograph remained of the library. From it, artists were able to plot the complicated geometric puzzle upon which the ceiling is based. Each finial was hand cast, and today the ceiling is in place. The single photo that made its reproduction possible hangs in the library today. The plasterwork and painting of the mansion's grand ballroom ceiling is worth a bit of a stiff neck, too: a central panel depicting a cloud-washed blue sky, framed in plaster swirls and surrounded by painted medallions.

If all these beautiful ceilings inspire you to add a little class (and more overhead) to your own mansion, help is at hand. The plasterwork in the billiard room at Rosecliff was recently restored from a 1910 photograph by a nearby Massachusetts firm, **Joshua & Co.** (508-789-3376, www.plasterart.com).

Although you'll see outstanding ceilings in all the mansions, possibly the most ornate ones are at **The Breakers**. The best view of the ceiling of the Great Hall is from the Loggia above, whose frescoed ceiling is no slouch itself. Carrying out a theme of an open wall overlooking the sea, the artist created a faux pavilion tent roof overhead.

SECRET
CHAPELS

❖

Founded in 1919, the **Seaman's Church Institute** (18 Market Square, at America's Cup Avenue, 847-4260) has ever since been a "haven for men and women of the sea" with its reading room, inexpensive lunch counter, garden, and 1929 Art Deco **Chapel by the**

Sea on the second floor. It's a bit difficult to find: go through the door in the left-hand wall of the library. It is a most unusual place, with a floor inlaid with seashells, and wall frescoes of the patron saints of fishermen. Carefully stitched needlepoint kneelers have designs drawn from the briny as well. What even the few people who find this quiet refuge often don't know is that the chapel was built so that it could be rolled up and carried off to the Naval War College if the mission of the institute ever changes. Floors come up, walls roll up and even the faux-marble ceiling, painted on canvas, can be carried away intact.

One of my favorite retreats is the almost-unknown **St. Columba's Chapel** (55 Vaucluse Avenue, off Peckham Road, Middletown, 847-5571). Built in 1884, this granite chapel has a small bell tower and a covered side portico. Stained glass by three of the foremost glass artists — Tiffany, John LaFarge, and Maitland Armstrong — fills the chapel with colored light. A memorial inside records the bravery of a West Point cadet. Outside, the church is surrounded by a lovely churchyard with interesting stones. An effigy tomb, some fine Celtic crosses with knotwork designs, and a lych gate are all unusual in America. It's as though a tiny English country church had been transplanted to the Rhode Island shore.

SECRET CHASM

If **Purgatory Chasm** (Tuckerman Road, off Purgatory Road from Memorial Drive, Middletown) were anywhere else, it would be a major tourist attraction, but Newport has so many of those that this gaping hole in the shore is left pretty much to the natives. One reason it may not get much press is the fear that people with more testosterone than brains might be tempted to climb into it. This would be a very silly thing to do, since the sudden rush of seawater against wet, slippery walls makes it very dangerous. But there is a full and perfectly safe view of all of it from the bridge that crosses one end. The chasm, formed by the force of the sea wearing away at a crack in the underlying stone, is about 10 feet wide and 50 feet deep. It is carved nearly 100 feet into the shore through the cliff. When the sea is high, water forcing itself into the narrowing channel makes a very loud noise.

SECRET
CHEAP LUNCH
✤

If you can't find a table in the simple dining room, you may find yourself at the counter of **The Green Galley** (Seaman's Church Institute, 18 Market Square, at Bowen's Wharf, 847-4260) between a businessman in a fine suit and a sea-worn fisherman put out of work by the moratorium. But you won't find a better value for breakfast or lunch than the restaurant's substantial portions of well-prepared comfort foods. Plump omelettes (renowned for their variety, with 15 choices of fillings in any combination), fresh-from-the-oven muffins, and the bacon-and-eggs usuals are served from 7 AM until 2 PM, along with homey soups, chowder, chili, and beans with coleslaw. The Portuguese sweet bread toast is heavenly. You can get a hearty bowl of soup and a sandwich for less than $5.

SECRET
CHIC
✜

Creamy vintage fabrics become dreamy dresses in the hands of the two talented designers at **Tatters** (36 Broadway, 841-0886). Carol and Geri make one-of-a-kind things to slip into for a night out, as well as more workaday creations that you still feel really sharp in. A good assortment of handbags and kids' clothes rounds out a thoroughly chic shop.

SECRET
CHOWDAH
✜

If you want to find out who makes chowder just the way you like it, step up to the pot at the annual **Chowder Cook-off** (Newport Yachting Center, Commercial Wharf, 846-1600) in June. Sample all 30 of the area's best chefs' versions, then go back for more of your favorite. The title for the best chowder is serious business, as it should be. You will find several variations here, and out-of-staters need to know that Rhode Island–style chowder uses no cream or milk — and certainly no tomatoes (which, of course, make a soup that is not chowder at all, but seafood soup pretending to be respectable).

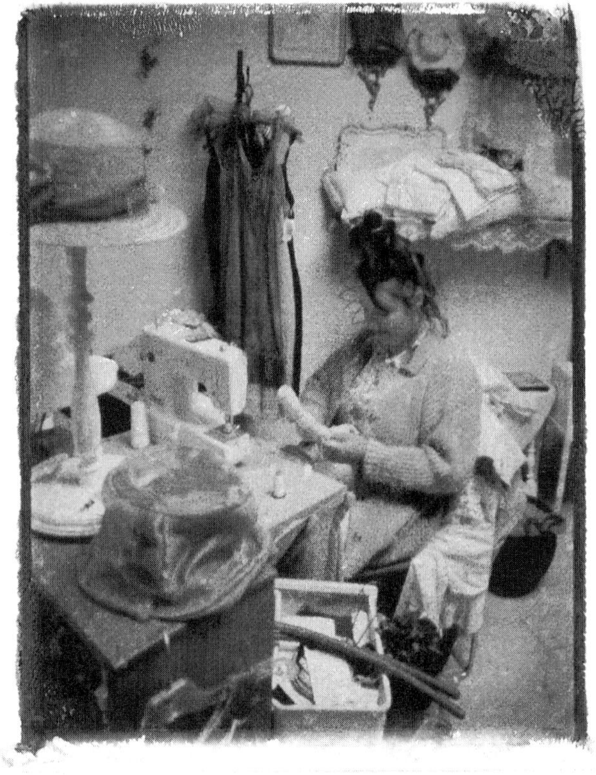

SECRET CHURCHES

Only two churches in America have full interiors decorated by the artist John LaFarge, and the **Newport Congregational Church** (Spring and Pelham streets, 849-2238) is one of them. Yet hardly anyone comes to see it — or even knows it's there. LaFarge was best known for his extraordinary stained glass, but rarely can you see his characteristic opalescent glass windows together with his wall and ceiling decorations. The paintwork, covering even the organ pipes, seems almost Byzantine, hardly what you would expect in a New England Congregational church. Newport's religious leanings were a far cry from the Puritanism that prevailed in the rest of New England. You can visit Tuesday and Thursday mornings in the summer, or by making an appointment, which is well worth the trouble.

Just up the hill is **Channing Memorial Church** (135 Pelham Street, 846-0643), another LaFarge masterpiece. He created the stunning memorial windows in the chancel of this red granite church, which was built to honor the founder of Unitarianism. You must make an appointment to visit, but, like the Congo church, it's well worthwhile. LaFarge, by the way, did not confine himself to church decoration; he also did the stained glass in the skylight above the grand staircase at The Breakers.

And while several private homes have fine stained glass, none visible from the street rivals that of nearby 601 Pelham Street, whose doorway looks like a kaleidoscope. Stroll past after dark to admire it; the owners keep it nicely lighted from within.

SECRET
CLIFF WALK

Most people do only the middle part of Cliff Walk, from Forty Steps to Marble House, doubling back to Marine Avenue, near Rosecliff, and returning along Bellevue Avenue. Even now that the walk's tunnel has been re-opened, few venture far beyond it. True, the middle section passes the major mansions, but we're rock-hoppers at heart, and love the part where the cliffs are wilder and the trail sometimes falls into the sea.

To walk the southern part all the way to Land's End, wear sturdy shoes and choose a day when it hasn't rained and the surf isn't high. Rough rocks are treacherous when they're wet. Parking is almost non-existent at Land's End, so you'll have to walk back.

At Marble House, right under the red Chinese Tea House, the trail goes through the tunnel, then disappears across a shingle beach. No mansions in sight here, just the sea and the rocky cliffs above. The east fronts of more estates come into view, then Rough Point, looking like something that should loom over Yorkshire in some Brontë novel. Those with vertigo will probably not enjoy crossing the deep chasm on a little footbridge (before you cross, make sure it's still there — it's sometimes lost in storms that lash this cliff). In the rock-strewn area beyond, look for big stones from a ruined cottage wall along the shore — part of an arch, a corbel, tide-tossed bricks. Forget looking for the trail and just pick your way along over the rocks in the last section, where Cliff Walk meets Ledge Road at Land's End. Return via Ledge Road to Bellevue Avenue for a west-front view of the same mansions.

SECRET COACHES
❦

A mile from The Breakers itself, **The Breakers Stable** (Coggeshall Avenue, at Bateman Avenue, 847-1000) is a brick stable and carriage house designed by the same architect as the house, to hold coaches, 28 horses, and their grooms. Inside are about 30 vehicles, including the Vanderbilt coach *Venture*, along with livery equipment and general Vanderbiltiana. The stable is open only in the summer. It's free with your mansion ticket, or you can get a ticket for the stable alone.

A **Weekend of Coaching** (847-1000), in August of even-numbered years, is a grand spectacle, as turn-of-the-century coaches are drawn down Bellevue Avenue by thoroughbred horses. Bellevue Avenue is closed to cars then, as it was in the heyday of the mansions (when it was closed by a gate to keep lesser folk from gaping through the fences). A similar coaching parade each afternoon during the Newport social season took the mistresses of the mansions for their ritualized afternoon ride. To arrive in style in your own horse-drawn carriage, call the **Newport Equestrian Center** (287 Third Beach Road, Middletown, 848-5440).

SECRET COFFEE
❦

The best thing about coffee in Newport is that S******k's hasn't moved into town and bought the buildings occupied by all the good coffee places. So you can still get a good cup of java. I'm an espresso drinker myself, so bear with me while I rant a bit about the tepid brown stuff that is put into an ice-cold cup and kept on the counter for 10 minutes in most restaurants. Not so at **Cheeky Monkey** (see "Secret Monkeys"), **Puerini's** (see "Secret Veal"), or **Asterix and Obelix** (see "Secret Fusion"). For plain old American coffee, the **Franklin Spa** (see "Secret Breakfasts") is popular. But for a serious wake-up call, I look to **Cappuccino's** (92 William Street, 846-7145), **The Market** (43 Memorial Boulevard, 848-2600), and **Espresso Yourself Cafe** (Perry Mill Market, 337 Thames Street and America's Cup Avenue, 847-1125).

SECRET COLONIAL

In all the glitter of the Gilded Age, Newport's colonial past gets forgotten. But when all that eye candy makes you a bit queasy, it's time for a spin around **The Point**, north of the visitors' center. This was the residential neighborhood for colonial ship captains, merchants, and ship owners. Washington Street is still lined with their homes, and in streets nearby are the homes and shops of the sail makers, cabinetmakers, shipbuilders, and others who outfitted the Newport ships. Washington Street had the finest homes in the colonies, and most of them are still there.

Hunter House (54 Washington Street, 847-1000) is not only one of the finest Colonial homes remaining in America; it is also furnished in outstanding works by early American cabinetmakers, some of the

COLONIAL 157

best of whom were from Newport. The decoration inside the house is extraordinary: five fully paneled rooms, including a parlor with faux marble around the fireplace and polychrome cherubs over the arched cupboard doors. The first block of Washington Street has several other mid-1700s buildings, and you can almost see the sailing ships that docked right behind the houses. Nearby Poplar Street is also lined with Colonial homes.

SECRET
CRAB CAKES
⁂

Don't believe for a minute that good crab cakes can't be made out of sight of Chesapeake Bay. **Quito's** (411 Thames Street, Bristol, 253-4500) is a waterfront seafood shop redolent of the seas, not of a deep fryer. I've never eaten anything I didn't like here, but I usually dive straight into one of their burly crab cakes, bigger than some hamburgers I've been served. Quito's is at the southern end of the East Bay Bike Path.

SECRET
CROWD CONTROL
⁂

Especially in high season and on weekends, the high-profile mansions are crowded, and you may have to wait in line for space on a tour. If you can't plan your visit for a quieter season or mid-week, you can at least control the crowds in your life somewhat by arriving when the mansions open in the morning, or at about 11:30 AM or noon. Why? It's an old truth of bus tours that people get cranky if they aren't real close to a place to eat by noon. So bus tours time their visits to get everyone back on the bus in time to hit lunch as the clock strikes 12. And the rest of us are beginning to flag by then, too, so it's usually the least-crowded time to arrive.

SECRET DEALS

Many visitors to Newport want to visit several mansions, and if your choices are those owned by the Preservation Society of Newport County, you can buy tickets for several combinations of mansions. In the same spirit, Belcourt Castle, Mrs. Astor's Beechwood, and the Tennis Hall of Fame offer a combined ticket at a reduced rate.

Look for ad hoc specials offered by restaurants and movie theaters, as well as combined offers from restaurants and the Newport Repertory Theatre. For dinner and legitimate theater, consider the Newport Playhouse, where one price includes a buffet dinner, the show, and a cabaret afterward.

Browse the racks of the visitors' center in the off season and midweek for frequent lodging deals. Look for special stickers on the brochures announcing rates that might be as low as $39 a night for one of the smaller B&Bs. Or before you go, visit Newport's tourism Web site (www.GoNewport.com) and click on the "Check This" feature to find the latest deals.

It costs $2 to cross the Newport (recently renamed Claiborne Pell) Bridge to Jamestown, but for $10 you can get a roll of 10 tokens, cutting the price in half.

SECRET
FINDS
✧

You never know what you'll find at the **Patriots' Shop** (73 Pelham Street, at Spring Street, no phone), located in the 1880s parish hall of the Newport Congregational Church. Previously owned fur stoles with beady little eyes, pillbox hats, tchotchkes from auntie's last vacation to Florida, sequined sweaters, last year's hemlines, Barbie dolls, unloved wedding gifts from faraway relatives... look for all those things that end up at thrift shops. You'll certainly find china, glassware, and other antiques and collectibles on consignment. It could be Waterford crystal or it could be K-Mart plastic, but I can't resist checking it every time I go by. It's the one-stop shop for all your neo-'70s needs.

Lily's of the Alley (64 Spring Street, 846-7545) doesn't have previously owned clothing, just previously shown. Again, there's no predicting what will be leftovers from the boutiques this season, but the prices will certainly beat the original ones.

SECRET
FISH
✤

Brightly colored tropical fish in New England waters? Right here in Newport, I swear to it. The warm summer and fall currents of the Gulf Stream bring such a startling array of fish from tropical waters that museum and aquarium staffs come here to collect them in the fall. It's actually a rescue mission, since it's a watery one-way street, and they would not survive the winter here.

Of course, this makes diving especially interesting, when coupled with the shipwrecks (some from the 1700s), ledges, and reefs to explore. And the water is clear. Try the rocky shore of Brenton Point State Park, the western shore of Beavertail State Park, or Fort Wetherill, near Jamestown, which has two sheltered, south-facing coves and a rocky drop-off. The **Newport Diving Center** (550 Thames Street, 847-9293 or 1-800-DIVING-0, www.newportdiving.com) gives lessons, provides diving gear, and makes regularly scheduled trips. **Ocean State Scuba** (at the pier, Jamestown, 423-1662 or 1-800-933-DIVE) also offers full diving services.

But you don't have to dive to see these bright little fish (actually, if they were really bright, they would have stayed home where the water stays warm). All the creatures at the **Newport Aquarium** (Easton's Beach, Memorial Boulevard, 849-1340) either grew up in Narragansett Bay or arrived by the Gulf Stream express. You can stick your hands into the touch tank and pat a shark (go ahead, Rhode Island sharks are harmless) or poke at a hermit crab, or you can watch the calamari hatch and grow bigger.

SECRET
FISH & CHIPS
❦

Cooking fish & chips is a much-neglected art. The fish needs to be fresh, the batter needs to be thin enough to crisp without burning while the fish cooks to just flaky inside, and the deep fryer needs to be at precisely the right temperature to keep the batter from absorbing fat. **The Red Parrot** (348 Thames Street, 847-3140) knows all this and is generous with its servings, too. You can barely squeeze into this place on a summer evening, or when the sounds of cool jazz waft into Thames Street on weekend nights, so go for the music then and the food any other time.

SECRET
FOLK ART
❦

If they changed the sign on **Cadeaux du Monde** (26 Mary Street, 848-0550) and took off the price tags, people would easily believe it to be a museum. Traditional artworks, handmade clothing, and folk crafts from Africa, Asia, and South and Central America very quickly turn browsing into temptation.

SECRET '40S

During World War II, Newport rocked — or more likely it reeled — with Navy presence. It was Sailortown USA, with ships coming and going and a steady stream of blue suits and white hats turning the town on its heels. Few of the old sailor haunts remain, although you can often get a glimpse of what it was like at the **Museum of Newport History** (Washington Square, at 127 Thames Street, 846-0813).

It's hard to picture now, but Goat Island, behind the visitors' center, was a torpedo station. Easier to imagine, since the ruins are still there, is the explosives storage and assembly station on Rose Island, where explosives were mixed and added to torpedoes.

Even the mansions were involved in the war effort, when Vanderbilt heiress Countess Szechenyi made the vast cellars at The Breakers available as an air raid shelter. She also donated all the huge copper cooking pots from the kitchens to the government to help relieve the copper shortage, which is why the pots you see there today don't have the Vanderbilt monogram. The current ones were donated to the Preservation Society of Newport County by owners of neighboring cottages.

Brenton Point State Park (Ocean Avenue, 846-8240) was a site for radar and anti-aircraft searchlights, with anti-torpedo-boat weapons. Look for the wide circular Panama gun mount near the parking lot. The park headquarters has information on the history of the property.

SECRET
FORTS

While the bulky silhouette of Fort Adams is hard to miss, Narragansett Bay's strategic importance has been so significant that Aquidneck Island is literally strewn with the remnants of fortifications dating from as early as colonial days. Rhode Island's only major battle of the Revolution was centered on **Butts Hill Fort** (Butts Street, off Sprague Street, Portsmouth) on August 29, 1778, as Americans tried to drive the British off the island. Although once maintained, the fort is now forgotten, overgrown with weeds and brush as trees begin to reclaim the earthworks. The stone entry is falling apart and the monument has been toppled, but in the fort's desolation, you can almost hear the little ragtag militia trying to figure out how to beat the best trained army of its day. This was the first battle that the first Black regiment in America ever fought in; a monument to the First Rhode Island Regiment, composed of freed Black and Indian slaves, is on the west side of Route 114 north, near its junction with Route 24.

The best preserved, and least known, fort is on Rose Island, close to the lighthouse and almost overgrown by vegetation. In remarkably good structural condition is a set of vaulted brick barracks constructed in 1798, when the island's fortification and earthworks were expanded as **Fort Hamilton**. Earthworks were first built here by the British; the French constructed more during the Revolution. Because nearly all the other First System Fortifications (as coastal defenses built in the early years of the United States are called) have been destroyed or seriously altered by later ones, the Rose Island barracks are especially important historically.

Fort Wetherill (East Shore Road, Jamestown, 423-9941 in summer or 884-2010 year round) was completed before the War of 1812, manned during the Civil War, and enlarged during the Spanish-American War. By the time of the world wars, it was fortified by seven batteries, with 16-foot thick walls, hidden in sand and vegetation, and plotting rooms and ammunition storage deep under them. Today, you can see many traces of gun emplacements from the two world wars. Hiking trails wind around the point, with views of Newport and Castle Hill.

On tours with the rangers at **Beavertail State Park** (Beavertail Road, Conanicut Island, 423-9941 in summer or 884-2010 year round), you can explore some of the old military buildings and underground facilities used during World War II. The ruins of others are still there, and left of the parking lot, east of the lighthouse, is the sealed-off bunker of Battery Whiting. Beyond is an observation station, with gun emplacements just outside.

SECRET
FREE MANSIONS

Of course, you have to pay admission to see the most famous of the Gilded Age mansions, but several of the lesser ones have been set to other uses, so you can look them over free. When I say lesser, that doesn't mean that they are without the same fine artistry of the pleasure palaces of the Vanderbilts and Astors. They just don't have so much of it. The headquarters of the **Preservation Society of Newport County** (424 Bellevue Avenue, 847-1000, ext. 158) are in the former Pell mansion, an 1880s stone home with a lovely rose garden. Outstanding inside the building is its long central foyer, with a frieze above the fine wood paneling surmounted by a series of beautifully carved faces, each different and each an Irish king.

Now used as the Senior Center, the **Edward King House** (Aquidneck Park, off King Street, 846-7426) offers weekday tours, but you can go in and look around anytime during business hours. It is a Gothic brownstone and brick, with Italianate trim and balconies. Like the Pell mansion, the main feature is the outstanding central hall.

The largest of this trio, **Ochre Court** (100 Ochre Point Avenue), is now the administration building for Salve Regina University, which occupies (and has saved) several other mansions in the neighborhood. More have been converted into classrooms and dormitories. Ochre Court looks like a Gothic-style French chateau, the design of Richard Morris Hunt. Ask at the reception desk for the free leaflet describing the building and its art. The three-story great hall becomes more elaborate and ornate as it rises floor by floor. The thing to see inside is the stained glass from the Spitzen collection, which looks its best in the morning with the sun shining through it. On weekends, when the building is closed, go around to the ocean-side terrace and look in the large windows to see the stained glass. Late afternoon is the best time to do this, because the sun shines through the west windows on the other side of the building. On the outside of the mansion is some wonderful Gothic detail on its pinnacles, and a sundial on the south chimney.

SECRET
FRIED CLAMS
❖

To get two Rhode Islanders to agree on anything is newsworthy, but when you get an almost unanimous opinion, you know the subject must be food and the place must be really, really good. So it's no secret that **Flo's Drive-In** (Park Avenue, off Route 138 near Island Park, Portsmouth, no phone) has the best fried clams on the island. They just don't get any better than Flo's. The other seafood — scallops, shrimp, fish filets — is given the same attention, and you can eat at picnic tables overlooking the water. It's only open in the summer.

SECRET
FUSION
❖

Anyone who would put a high-taste restaurant in an old garage has the right mindset for the unpredictable contrasts of fusion cooking. **Asterix and Obelix** (599 Lower Thames Street, 841-8833) takes full advantage of the building's architectural quirks in the summer, when the staff opens the big roll-up front doors (converted to glass) so the dining room flows European-style into the sidewalk cafe. Mediterranean mingles, merges, and plays with Asian in some dishes, while remaining distinct in others. Swordfish might be sautéed with roasted macadamia nuts and served in a Thai curried lobster sauce, accompanied by Chinese greens. No fusion in the pâté, though — it's classic French, judiciously laced with cognac. The cafe offers an eclectic breakfast and brunch menu daily, everything from a full English breakfast to potato gallette. You'll need dinner reservations in the summer.

SECRET GARDENS

Thousands of people walk right by the tiny garden of the **Seaman's Church Institute** (18 Market Square, at America's Cup Avenue, 847-4260) without even knowing it's there. Hidden inside its walls, the quiet little oasis was planted in memory of those who "challenged wind and sail in pursuit of a dream." A model fishing boat is set into its brick wall. Shady and cool in the summer, it hardly seems like it's in the middle of the busiest spot in Newport.

At the **Wanton-Lyman-Hazard House** (15 Broadway, near Washington Square, 846-0813), a museum house operated by the Newport Historical Society, the kitchen garden has been restored, with herbs, flowers, and vegetables that would have been grown by an upper-middle-class merchant in colonial times.

Turn an enthusiastic gardener loose on even a small piece of earth and there's no end to what he can create. The not-extensive yard of **The Victorian Ladies** (63 Memorial Boulevard, 849-9960) proves that. Flowers climb the fences, repose against the walls, and would probably cascade across the driveway, if Donald had his way. You can see the gardens from the street — or by walking into the driveway — but my favorite way to enjoy them is to look down on them from the charming little sitting-room alcove of Room 2, upstairs. Donald

GARDENS

and Helene run a classy little B&B, and, along with growing beautiful flowers, Donald cooks a mean breakfast. Guest rooms are decorated in deep forest green and warm burgundy, which highlight Helene's collections of fine antique needlework. A bonus secret: you can walk to Easton's Beach or the start of Cliff Walk from here, saving the $10 parking fee and a big headache in the summer.

On a Friday and Saturday in mid-June, you get a rare chance to see behind the fences and into the hidden backyards of The Point and other neighborhoods during **Secret Garden Tours** (847-0514). Between 15 and 20 gardens of private homes — gardens not open to the public otherwise — are shown at their height of bloom.

In April and May, the **Blithewold Mansion and Gardens** (Ferry Road, near Mount Hope Bridge, 253-2707) welcome spring with thousands of blooming bulbs. They cover the elegant grounds with yellow and white daffodils that herald the stunning displays of later spring and summer. These summer gardens may not be a secret, but no one who loves flowers should pass them by.

To pamper your own garden (or maybe your hands after working in it), depend on **Devonshire English Garden Shop** (304 Thames Street, at Prospect Hill Street, 847-4280). It's amazing how much they can show in this small shop without the place ever seeming busy or cramped — you can tell it is arranged by a gardener. High-quality British trowels, forks and hoes, baskets and trugs for collecting the bounty, thatched bird houses, pots, gardeners' hand soaps, and tasteful home decor items with a garden theme, as well as a good selection of gardening books, make the shop useful. In the winter, it is open only on weekends.

SECRET GLASS

❧

Matthew Buechner's designs turn glass into objects so delicate I half expect them to pop at a touch, like strings of bubbles from a wand. At **Thames Glass** (688 Thames Street, 846-0576) you can watch Matthew and his associates transform blobs of glowing molten glass into fragile perfume bottles, colorful paperweights, fruit bowls, or vases. I can't leave without a new addition to add a swirling burst of glowing color to my Christmas tree. Particularly appropriate to Newport are the schools of brilliant glass fish, echoing the colors of the tropical fish that visit local waters via the Gulf Stream (see "Secret Fish"). I'm not much for objets d'art, but even I can be tempted by these high-class doodads.

SECRET GRAVES

❧

One of the first places you'll pass as you arrive in Newport from the Newport Bridge is **Common Ground** (Farewell Avenue), laid out in the 1660s. Its oldest section, in the back (turn onto Warren Street, then left to enter near the chapel), holds row on crooked row of slate headstones, possibly New England's largest collection of early stones. Most face south, a boon for photographers, since many show winged little moon-faced cherubs or grinning skulls. The stones are in good condition and on many of them are quaint little verses or long lists of the departed's virtues. And no, the name of the street is not a coincidence — to be brought here was the last farewell.

Island Cemetery is a later addition, separated by a fence, near which you'll find an obelisk inside an iron fence containing the graves of Oliver Hazard Perry and Matthew Perry. (Oliver died in Trinidad and his remains were repatriated by an Act of Congress in 1824.) Opposite the Perry plot, you're brought suddenly into modern reality by a stark black granite stone in front of a large, newly planted plot. "Egypt Air Flight 990" is the only thing inscribed; no dates, no names. The rescue and recovery efforts for that air disaster were coordinated out of Newport.

Toward the center of Island Cemetery is a tomb marked with a standing angel sculpted by Augustus Saint-Gaudens. Nearby is the circular "Travers Pie," an unusual plot (but not the only one known) where a family is buried in circular fashion around the tomb of an ancestor.

An hour or so of wandering in this large cemetery will turn up more secrets, but Newport has several other small plots of almost forgotten graves. Below Touro Park on Pelham Street, beside the imposing pillars of a large white house, is the burial place of Benedict Arnold, the first governor of Rhode Island (and ancestor of the traitor with the same name), along with touchingly tiny slate markers for several of his children, one only 17 days old. Two of the larger slate stones have winged skulls.

More early governors repose for eternity in **Clifton Burial Ground** (Golden Hill Street, off Spring Street), along with Roger Williams's daughter, Mary. The stones, with sculls and angel heads, date mostly from the 1600s.

In the churchyard of **Trinity Church** (Queen Anne's Square, 846-0660) are buried Admiral de Ternay, commander of the French naval forces that had their headquarters here after the occupation, and

General Lafayette's aide-de-camp. Both men were Catholic, and there was no Catholic parish or cemetery in Newport, so a section of Trinity's churchyard was specially consecrated for them.

SECRET
GREEK
❦

St. Spyridon's Greek Orthodox Church (390 Thames Street, at Brewer Street, 846-0555), just before the Francis Malbone House, has a wonderful festival in July each year in the parking lot adjacent to the church. It's a lively day of Greek music, dancing, traditional crafts, games, and family activities. But best of all is the food. This is a rare chance to sample real baklava, made from old family recipes (don't even try to compare it to the pale shadows of it served in most restaurants). Plan on a lunch of succulent lamb, skewers of kebabs, salads redolent of real olives, and feta cheese. Makes my mouth water just writing about it.

Nikolas Pizza (38 Memorial Boulevard West, 849-6611) serves, along with the obvious pizza, Greek specialties — and wicked hot wings (not Greek, but good).

SECRET
HISTORY
❦

Here's another museum you can sleep in, but at the other end of the luxury scale from a lighthouse. **The Francis Malbone House**

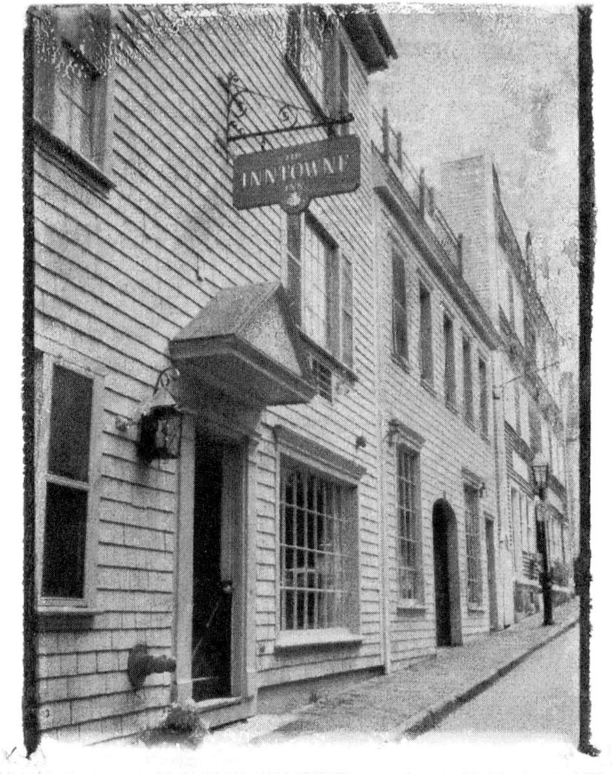
INNTOWNE

(392 Thames Street, 846-0392), a meticulously restored 1760 shipowner's mansion, is one of only two remaining of those that once lined Lower Thames. Adjoining is an 1860 counting house, gently converted to a suite. In the two drawing rooms are comfortable chairs, books, games, and magazines, and guest rooms are elegantly, although simply, dressed in period antiques and fine reproductions. The fireplaces are real, and they work. In the midst of all this authenticity, breakfasts are authentically up to date, with hot dishes, fresh fruit, and baked goods. After dinner (the Malbone is in the midst of Restaurant Row), it's nice to step through the impressive front door — and back a couple of centuries.

SECRET HOOCH

Moving goods from boats and into hiding without any officials taking notice was a long-held tradition in Newport. The Francis Malbone House (see "Secret History") had a tunnel straight from the docks to its cellars, and it's doubtful that the king's agents ever saw the most taxable of Malbone's cargoes. So when Prohibition hit town, Newport was prepared. Add to that the demand — quite a few of the society families still summered here, and you can be sure they weren't serving tea at their parties — and you have the stage set for rum running.

You can learn all about it on a cruise aboard ***Rumrunner II*** (849-3033), one of the boats that engaged in this lucrative trade (under a less obvious name, of course). Sleek and fast, these classic wooden motor yachts played hide-and-seek with the Feds and delivered contraband

SECRET
IRISH
✧

Irish immigrants provided much of the labor that built the Newport mansions, as well as the staff that kept them running. In the evening, after the long days of work were over, the stonemasons, gardeners, chambermaids, and footmen would gather at **Forty Steps** (at the end of Narragansett Street) to socialize, romance, and sing a few songs of the Auld Sod. Today, you can hear genuine Irish music at one of New England's truest Irish pubs, **Aiden's Pub** (1 Broadway, 845-9311). Baskets of flowers hang out front, and as you enter you can almost believe you're on Grafton Street in Dublin. Wednesdays and Saturdays are usually seisun nights.

Newport's population is about 65 percent Irish, except during the **St. Patrick's Day Parade** (849-8048 or 1-800-326-6030, www.GoNewport.com), when you'd swear it was 110 percent. The parade, about 40 years old, is one of the oldest continuously held in the country. It follows the green stripe along Broadway and Thames Street to its far end, an area known as the "Fifth Ward" that was the traditional heart of the old Irish neighborhood.

In fact, all of March is **Irish Heritage Month** (849-8048 or 1-800-326-6030, www.GoNewport.com), with citywide activities celebrating Celtic culture and traditions with folk singers, step dancing, and other performers. In March, the street in front of St. Augustine's

Church, the Irish parish, is painted green. September brings an **Irish Music Festival**, with performing artists, Irish art, dance, poetry, crafts, foods, and storytelling.

SECRET
ITALIAN
✤

Although many of the most skilled artists who created the wood-and-stucco embellishments for Newport's mansions were Italian, no place shows them off better than two rooms at the French-named **Chateau-sur-Mer** (Bellevue Avenue, between Leroy and Shepard avenues, 847-1000). While the rest of the house is pure Arts and Crafts, by name designers like Eastlake and Morris, the library and dining room are gloriously Italian, designed, carved, and painted by Luigi Frullini. Leather was embossed, then gilded to cover the dining room walls, and the floor is intricately patterned in inlaid wood. Library furniture is heavily carved, set among rich wood bookcases under an ornate ceiling. Instead of being gloomy and ponderous, the setting makes me want to pull a book off the shelf and settle in.

For a taste of Bologna, travel no farther than the informal dining room of **Lucia** (186 Thames Street, 847-6355), where the chef has updated some of the best traditional dishes for New World dietary sensibilities. In short, he holds back on the fats, but not on the flavor. Vegetables are beautifully prepared — I usually order a sampler as an antipasto — and the menu has several good choices for vegetarians.

On a different note, **Trattoria Simpatico** (13 Narragansett Avenue, Jamestown, 423-3731) is all about the total perfect dining experience.

All is carefully orchestrated, from the Puccini arias — never too loud — to the choice of different china for presenting each dish. The service is right up there with the food, which speaks well for both. I have rarely begun dinner on a better note than the prosciutto-wrapped grilled asparagus over fresh garden greens I was served there one spring evening. Several nice wines are available by the glass, in case you and your partner can't agree on a bottle.

Newport celebrates all things Italian in mid-October at **Festa Italiana** (849-8048 or 1-800-326-6030), with art exhibits, *bel canto* performances, and an *abondanza* of food and wine. It all builds up to the Columbus Day parade.

SECRET JAPANESE

As a seafaring town, Newport had unique ties with Asian ports that were the destinations of ships in the lucrative China Trade, but none is so enduring as its ties with Japan. It was a local boy, Matthew Perry, whose 1853 visit opened Japan's long- and tightly closed doors to the outside world, beginning Western trade with Japanese ports. He landed at Bannister's Wharf on his return, and this event is celebrated annually at the **Black Ships Festival** (846-2720, www.NewportEvents.com) in late July. Demonstrations and workshops fill the weekend with kites, martial arts, Japanese brush painting, tea ceremonies, and Sumo wrestling. Newport has a continuing and active cultural exchange with its Japanese sister city, Shimoda.

You can see and buy museum-quality silk kimono, embroidery, and fans at **Norton's Oriental Gallery** (415 Thames Street, 849-4468).

It specializes in restoration and conservation of antique Asian textiles, and the shop is a gallery of fine examples.

I thought about a separate category in Newport just for sushi lovers, called "Secret Sushi," but these two restaurants serve much more. **Sea Shai** (747 Aquidneck Avenue, Middletown, 848-5180) — actually a Korean restaurant — serves the expected tempura and sukiyaki, but adds my own favorite, steaming thick bowls of good old peasant nabe, along with kushi-yaki, shabu-shabu, and several Korean dishes.

For bento lunches (or dinners, for that matter), stop at **Hisae's** (21 Valley Road [Route 214], Middletown, 848-6263). Bento lunches are not very expensive and include miso soup, yakisoba, hyashi-somen noodles, and a choice from a list of more substantial dishes, such as tempura squid rings. Dinner bento entrees are chosen from an even longer list. Between the sushi-maki and sushi-nigiri, Hisae offers nearly 30 sushi varieties.

SECRET
JAZZ
※

In the town that put jazz on the northern map with its legendary annual **Newport Jazz Festival** (847-3700), you can hear it played somewhere nearly any night of the week — at least in the summer.

The **Newport Blues Cafe** (286 Thames Street, 848-2105) rings with live blues and jazz Thursday through Sunday, usually beginning about 9 PM. Your eyes get a treat here, as well as your ears. The slightly domed ceiling of this reclaimed bank is deep cobalt blue, scattered with golden stars. The colors are echoed in a blue carpet and banquette upholstery, finished off by a dark wood bar and brass appointments. While admiring the stunning setting, you can choose from more than 60 wines by the glass or a large selection of ales.

The Red Parrot (348 Thames Street, at Memorial Boulevard, 847-3140) has live jazz every weekend, year round. Other places to check are the **Atlantic Beach Club** (53 Purgatory Road, Middleton, 847-2750), the **Rhode Island Quahog Company** (250 Thames Street, 848-2330), **Asterix and Obelix** (599 Thames Street, 841-8833), **Trattoria Simpatico** (13 Narragansett Avenue, Jamestown, 423-3731), and **The Lobster Pot** (119 Hope Street [Route 114], Bristol, 253-1900).

SECRET
JEWELRY

Estate jewelry, some of it from some pretty posh sources, is often consigned at **The Griffon Shop** (Newport Art Museum, 76 Bellevue Avenue, 848-8200). You may find other Newport treasures here, too, such as small antiques and collectibles. You don't have to pay museum admission to visit the shop. **Euphoria!** (411 Thames Street, 846-2290) also deals in estate jewelry, along with amber, and unusual gold and silver work.

Hardly a secret, but it seems a sin to mention jewelry in Newport without adding **J.H. Breakell, Silversmith** (132 Spring Street, 849-3522 or 1-800-767-6411), who designs and makes sterling and 14-karat gold jewelry at his studio. He often takes his inspiration from the sea, and is known for his beautiful and graceful silver sailboats. In his workshop on Spring Street, he and his assistants create each piece using the lost wax method, which has been used for casting precious metals since ancient times. Here's a secret, though: stop at the visitors' center to pick up his brochure, which may entitle you to a discount.

SECRET
JONNYCAKES
❖

A uniquely Rhode Island food (for such a small state, it has a lot of its own food traditions), the jonnycake is a small flapjack made with the ground meal of a particular kind of corn. Not many people grow it and fewer grind it, so real jonnycakes are hard to find. But every spring, usually on the Saturday closest to May 1, firemen, Rotary clubs, churches, and other local public service groups in communities all over the state put on May Breakfasts. And they always serve jonnycakes. Don't miss them. In Jamestown, it's the **Rotary Club Annual May Breakfast** (728-5400).

SECRET
JUDAICA
❖

North America's oldest Jewish house of worship, **Touro Synagogue** (85 Touro Street, 847-4794), was founded in 1763 by Spanish and Portuguese Jews, who chose Newport for its religious tolerance,

182   SECRET NEWPORT

notably missing in Puritan colonies to the north. Inside, the sanctuary is surrounded on three sides by balconies set on 12 finely detailed columns. All original, it is one of the finest interiors of its period in America. The oldest Torah in the United States, dating from the late 1400s, is here. George Washington visited the synagogue twice, once presenting a letter guaranteeing Jews religious freedom in the new United States. A copy is engraved on a plaque in the garden beside the building.

While the synagogue's significance to both Jewish and American history is certainly not a secret, many who come here are unaware of other related places in town. Farther up Touro Street is the Jewish Cemetery, dating from 1677, some stones so old that there is no sign of an inscription. Across from the **Common Ground** cemetery (Farewell Avenue, see "Secret Graves") is a section with more early Jewish graves. The papers, account books, and records of Aaron Lopez and other early Jewish merchants are maintained by the **Newport Historical Society** (82 Touro Street, 846-0813, see "Secret Ancestors").

S E C R E T
KIDS' STUFF
⚜

If you think your feet get tired trudging through miles of mansions, imagine how many more steps kids have to take to keep up — and they are rarely impressed, except by **Belcourt Castle** (see "Secret Astral Bodies"). But apart from mansions, Newport has a lot to interest kids. The **Newport Aquarium** (see "Secret Fish") is a good place to begin, especially if you hit the last weekend in September for the Setting Free Party. All the kids pitch in with buckets to help the aquarium return all their creatures to the sea.

The **Museum of Newport History** (Washington Square, at 127 Thames Street, 846-0813) has labels designed to involve children in its displays, set at their eye level. They can take printed sheets with them and follow the maps to find places relating to themes that interest them.

Summer **Children's Nights** (847-6875), every Tuesday and Thursday at 6:30 PM, include free programs at Easton's Beach. Newport has several other special events for kids, including the July **KidsFest** (846-1398). The **Black Ships Festival** (see "Secret Japanese"), in July, has special children's events, such as a sumo workshop for kids. **Haunted Newport** (845-9123, www.hauntednewport.com) fills the area with spooky doings that kids are bound to like. December brings **Christmas in Newport** (849-6454, www.christmasinnewport.org) and its events for children, with storytelling and other activities. **Opening Night** (842-0134) programs on New Year's Eve are earlier than those in most places, with fireworks beginning at 9:15 PM.

Newport is a pretty informal town, and children are welcome in most restaurants. The **Music Hall Cafe** (250 Thames Street, 848-2330), along with an adult menu of southwest grilled dishes, ribs, and TexMex specialties, has a children's menu at both lunch and dinner.

Modern suites at **Bay Voyage** (150 Conanicus Avenue, Jamestown, 423-2100 or 1-800-225-3522) are good for families, with separate bedrooms and kitchenettes equipped for preparing meals. The resort has a swimming pool and a program for children, who will like the inn's own secret: the whole building was floated to Jamestown on a barge.

SECRET KITCHEN

The enormous kitchen at The Breakers is unusual because it is not beneath the house in the basement, but on ground level in a separate el. This was because Mr. Vanderbilt feared that a fire in one of the enormous stoves could engulf the house before it could be stopped. The first mansion on this site had burned flat, so he was adamant that as much of the house as possible be fireproof. Even the heating system is in a separate building that doubled as the gatekeeper's cottage. The giant stove in the kitchen cooked three meals a day for the entire household and their guests, plus a staff of 40, in addition to parties that routinely numbered 200 at dinner. The pantries are filled with daily utensils, as well as the family china, by Meissen and others. So vast was the collection that it was actually stored on a mezzanine, carried there by a dumbwaiter after it was washed and polished. When your pantry needs a second level, you have too many dishes.

If you don't have too many dishes, **Runcible Spoon** (180 Bellevue Avenue, 849-3737) sells glass, china, and painted ceramics. If there's a kitchen gadget they don't have, you don't need it. A tasting table tempts you with pricey new delicacies. Specialty foods and cookbooks round it out as the ultimate one-stop kitchen store.

SECRET KITES

✤

On a breezy Saturday or Sunday, the sky above Brenton Point State Park is usually aswirl with kites of every color. Year round, a sunny day usually means kites, since the point is rarely without wind. Brenton Point is the venue, too, for the annual **Newport Kite Festival** (846-3262, www.buyakite.com), held in early July. The lift is excellent here, but when the water becomes too cool for swimming, you'll also see kites on the beaches. To buy a kite or a new reel of string, go to **High Flyers Flight Co.** (492 Thames Street, 846-3262).

SECRET LOBSTERS

✤

Inside the plain gray building of **Aquidneck Lobster** (Bowen's Wharf, 846-0106) are more than 5,000 live lobsters bound for restaurants all over North America. The plain doors may not make it look as though you're invited inside, but you are quite welcome. The interior boggles the mind. Lobsters are sorted into large tanks by size, and someone will be glad to hold up the lobsters-of-unusual-size, which may run 20 or 30 pounds. Consider that a standard dinner-plate pound-and-a-halfer is about 10 years old and guess how old some of these guys are. You'd probably be wrong, but if they ask you to guess, surprise them by suggesting about 100 to 150 years old, depending on the size. Actually, these big ones aren't all that tasty, and anything over five pounds is headed for the bisque pot, which I think is a shame, when these venerable examples could have been tossed back into the sea. Having grown up around lobster traps, I still can't imagine how some of these giants manage to get through the "door" to get caught, and I keep meaning to ask.

You may be surprised to see lobsters that are green and others that are orange, as well as calico shells or a rare albino or blue lobster. And be sure to note the difference between right- and left-handed lobsters. The place smells — not surprisingly — like lobster, and the floor is wet, since this is a busy working distribution center.

To see the catch brought in and unloaded from the boats, come early in the morning. It's easy to forget, in the glitter of the mansions and the sleek lines of the pleasure yachts, that Newport is still at its heart a working port.

SECRET MANSIONS

Of course, these mansions are as well advertised as any, and open to the public, but only those people who have been to Newport many times seem to visit them, opting for the more famous and lavish ones first. But I think these little-known mansions are some of the most interesting. **Kingscote** (Bellevue Avenue, at Bowrey Street, 847-1000) is the oldest of the mansions, built in 1841. Although it predates the ostentation-for-its-own-sake craze that followed, Kingscote began the grand annual social migration to Newport. Its owner came from Savannah each summer, not for high society, of which there was none, but for the simple outdoor pleasures and cooler temperatures. But as the Civil War grew imminent, things got hotter in Newport for southern slave owners, and Kingscote was sold to a family that would spend summers there until the 1970s. This unique and century-long single ownership kept the house from being torn down for development — it wasn't for sale — and ensured that the original furnishings from the mid-1800s remained. The contents were accumulated by a major family in the China Trade and include one of the finest private collections of Chinese paintings in America.

The best-known feature, a dining room the size of a ballroom, was added in the 1870s, with a delicate screen of carved spindles and an entire wall of Tiffany glass bricks and tiles. It's the only house that bridges the gap between colonial Newport and the Gilded Age, and you could picture actually living here.

Rough Point (Bellevue Avenue, 849-7300) is certainly the most secretive of the mansions that are open to view. Its heavy gates open only to admit the bus carrying a limited number of visitors, who have reserved and boarded at the visitors' center. You don't just drop in on Doris Duke's house when you're in the neighborhood and, until quite recently, no visitors had seen any more than its impressive red sandstone exterior. Like Kingscote, it was built to live in, and as a home for the extensive range of art that Doris Duke's father, Frederick Vanderbilt, had collected. It was not built, as the others were, for lavish parties and for show, although nothing was spared in adorning it with the finest workmanship and materials, from hand-painted Chinese wallpapers to deeply sculptured plaster ceilings. There is a finesse — you might say taste — to it that is missing in most of the others, and its art collections class it as a first-rate museum as well.

Portraits and other paintings by Van Dyke, Gainsborough, Reynolds, del Vecchio, and Renoir, 15th-century Ming porcelains, a Jacobean chest, an embroidered silk couch from a French chateau, silver and ivory tables made for Catherine the Great, Brussels and Aubusson tapestries... the list goes on. In Doris Duke's bedroom, alongside tiny childhood trophies for tennis, tango, and sandcastle building, is an amazing suite of furniture inlaid with mother-of-pearl, considered to be the most important decorative art collection in the house.

In a hallway is a reliquary, complete with the bones of a saint whose identity remains secret, and in a coatroom off the front hall, on the way to the ladies' room, is a simply exquisite example of padded embroidery. Often called stumpwork, the figures on this example have minutely stitched, freestanding hands. You should ask to see it, since it's a rare opportunity to appreciate a piece of this rarity at such close range.

SECRET
MILL

The enigmatic **Old Stone Mill** (Touro Park, Bellevue Avenue and Pelham Street) keeps its secrets well. Who built it, when, and even why have been subject to speculation for centuries. The Vikings? Probably not, although there are those who swear to it as staunchly as though they'd been there to watch the long prows bobbing in the harbor. I have a theory that this is the secret shibboleth by which you can distinguish the real Newporters from Johnny-come-lately types. Ask about the mill and old timers will tell you emphatically that the Vikings built it.

So who really did? Possibly Benedict Arnold, first governor of Rhode Island, who wrote about building a stone windmill. Analysis of the mortar suggests this period, but some other evidence suggests that it's older. The early Portuguese explorers have been mentioned. In fact, everyone except Elvis has been mentioned. This subject will be explored in greater detail in my next book, to be entitled *Unidentified and Mysterious Stone Things in Rhode Island*, of which this is but one.

SECRET MONKEYS

The monkey tradition in Newport probably predates even the Gilded Age host who dressed a monkey in full formal attire and made it guest of honor at a society dinner. The housewarming of The Elms was the largest party of the 1901 season; three orchestras played, and a troupe of trained monkeys was released to perform in the park. Some escaped and were never retrieved, but for quite some time monkeys were seen around town.

One of the city's many excellent public artworks is a bronze monkey in the garden of Brick Market Place. This monkey works for a living, collecting money in his bronze cup for battered women's programs. While he's out working, his tony cousins relax in the convivial atmosphere of **The Cheeky Monkey** (14 Perry Mill Wharf, 845-9494, www.cheekymonkey.com). Their portraits smile down approvingly on the smartly decorated dining room. After looking at them for a while on one visit, we began to realize why they looked familiar. The knowing gentleman on the end wall looked remarkably like George Burns, and the matron above our table bore an uncanny resemblance to Rose Kennedy. You can join more monkeys upstairs in a more secret room with soft couches, designed for savoring a quiet glass of cognac after dinner. If there's not a private party going on, look into the room across the hall to see Queen Elizabeth and a human-sized painted wood sculpture of a smartly dressed monkey in a uniform complete with epaulets, brass buttons, and medals. The Generalissimo is clearly El Presidente of . . . you guessed it, a Banana Republic. Cheeky indeed.

But the monkey business stops short of the menu. The chef and owner are very serious about the food. The chef delights in serving tasting menus, where you can sample several dishes. He serves them elegantly on a tiered platter like an English tea tray, set in the center so everyone can easily sample each dish without going through the messy (and often hazardous) business of plate or fork swapping. Seared salmon crusted in black sesame seeds might be served with baby corn, a carrot gaufrettte, and shaved pickled ginger. The lobster ravioli is not just the usual pasta pocket of lobster paste; fat chunks of tender lobster hide inside, and the ravioli are served in a light cream sauce with a hint of curry. No compromises here. If the tuna isn't the first one off the boat, it's crossed off the menu. Full servings are generous, which is another reason to opt for the tasting menu and be able to enjoy more than a single course. Impresario Maggie Gordon is clearly on the cutting edge with this restaurant, and it's very popular, so you'll want a reservation.

SECRET MOVIES

※

If you're an old movie fan, some of the mansions may look familiar. They've been used in a lot of movies, including *The Great Gatsby*, which was filmed at Rosecliff in 1974, as was *The Betsy* with Laurence Olivier. *High Society* (Grace Kelly, Bing Crosby, Frank Sinatra, and Louis Armstrong) was filmed at Clarendon Court, and begins with aerial shots of Newport and the mansions. *The Bostonians* used the sitting room at Chateau-sur-Mer, as did BBC's production of Edith Wharton's *The Buccaneers*.

Arnold Schwarzenegger stayed at nearby **Ivy Lodge** (12 Clay Street, 849-6865) while filming *True Lies* in 1994 at Ochre Court. Ivy Lodge is one of the few lodgings right in the mansion neighborhood. Stanford White designed it and upstairs hallways are balconies above a richly paneled central entry hall. I like Room 1, with a fireplace and an amazing oak bed. Breakfast is bountiful, served with crystal and silver. Bicycles, beach towels, and chairs are provided to guests.

Newport's favorite silver screen is at the **Jane Pickens Theater** (49 Touro Street, Washington Square, 846-5252), built in 1836 as Zion Episcopal Church. It was a burlesque house in flapper days, switching to movies when the talkies bumped out burlesque. The screen is huge, the sound system state of the art.

SECRET MURDERS

A scream echoes from the ballroom and guests rush to find Trixie standing over dead Eddie... but later, he gets up to join his fellow actors and guests over punch and cookies. These aren't murders of the real kind — although Claus von Bulow, just up the street, was tried for the murder of his wife Sunny. These are pretend murders staged by the actors who populate **Mrs. Astor's Beechwood** (580 Bellevue Avenue, 846-3772), who on non–Murder Mystery days always greet guests at the door and escort them through the mansion, sharing equal measures of gossip and history that illuminate the lifestyle of the Astors and their fellow socialites. Whoever escorts you, you'll hear plenty about *the* Mrs. Astor, doyenne of New York society at the close of the 19th century and arbiter of who was who. Tour themes change frequently, and you may meet an Irish maid who will tell part of Beechwood's story from a backstairs point of view, or a member of the family or a "fellow guest" at a weekend house party. Tours usually end with a re-enactment of a musicale, with a short course on proper etiquette at a house party, or with instructions on the proper use of a fan for flirting.

It has nothing to do with murders, but Cole Porter finished the song "Night and Day" at Beechwood, having begun it on the banks of the Rhine. Vincent, son of John Jacob Astor IV, was one of Porter's friends.

SECRET MUSEUMS

Anywhere but Newport, the **Samuel Whitehorne House** (416 Thames Street, 847-2448) would join Hunter House (see "Secret Colonial") as a major draw, but here it's barely known. After a full restoration, the city's finest example of a Federal period home is now much as it was when it was built, in 1811. The furnishings comprise one of New England's finest collections — more than a dozen pieces made by or attributed to the colonial cabinetmakers Townsend and Goddard, along with colonial pewter, silver, and china. So many

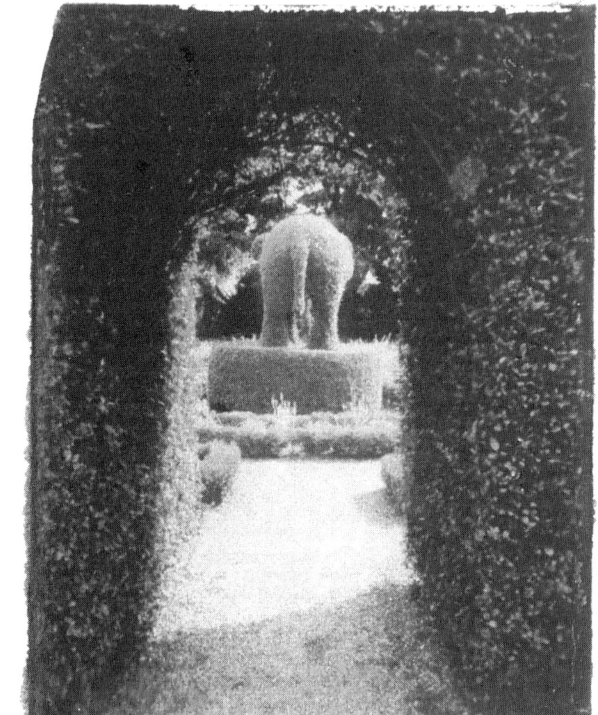

priceless examples fill this house that guides point out only a few of the best for fear of wearing you out. If you're especially interested in furniture, or other subjects, tell the guide at the beginning of the tour, so she can make sure you see the best examples. Hidden behind the house is a beautiful period garden; the best view of its design is from a second-floor window.

Across the harbor in Jamestown, finds from an archaeological dig at a 3,000-year-old Native American burial site are shown at the free **Sydney L. Wright Museum** (Jamestown Philomenian Library, 26 North Road, Jamestown, 423-2665). Artifacts here represent the island from its earliest human habitation through the settlement by Europeans. Well displayed, the collection contains an ancient ax head, other stone implements, and a Narragansett basket from the 1600s.

Although its topiary gardens are its main attraction, **Green Animals** (Cory's Lane, off Route 114, Portsmouth, 847-1000) is also an outstanding museum of Victorian toys. Most people who visit the gardens don't even know it's there, but inside the house you'll find a puppet theater, dolls, toy soldiers, and moving tin toys. Special Christmas programs show off the collections around the holidays.

SECRET
NECESSITIES

Along the Newport waterfront, you'll find public restrooms in the visitors' center, at the Mary Street parking lot (although they are open only in the summer), and at the Seaman's Church Institute. Elsewhere in town, they are scarce.

SECRET
NEW AMERICAN
✤

The last place you'd think to look for a creative New American menu is in a place that's as quintessentially early American as the **Nathaniel Porter Inn** (125 Water Street, Warren, 245-6622). The house was built in the 1700s and has been beautifully restored, with three antique-furnished guest rooms. But the restaurant, for all its colonial ambiance, serves 100 percent New American cuisine — and does a splendid job of it.

SECRET
OASIS
✤

When natives want a moment's peace from the fast pace of summer along the waterfront, they slip into the quiet refuge of **The Pineapple Grill** (Hyatt Regency Hotel, Goat Island, 851-1234). The bar overlooks the pool, nestled in pine trees, with a 180-degree view of the Newport Bridge. Relax on a cedar chair under an umbrella and order a bucket of steamers or choose from the menu of about 10 items, mostly grilled. America's Cup Avenue is suddenly at least five miles away.

SECRET
OYSTERS
❖

Redolent of the sea, as oysters ought to be, are the mollusks at the **Jamestown Oyster Bar and Grill** (22 Narragansett Avenue, Jamestown, 423-3380). This plain-Jane place may be full of local fishermen (a good clue right there) or tanned yachtsmen fresh from a race — or a mix of both, all slurping their oysters without formality. The fish & chips is good, too. You can walk from the ferry landing, a block away.

SECRET
PACK RATS
❖

At the end of a long driveway, marked on Route 136 by a single sign, Brown University hides an amazing treasure house of collections that encompass everything from local native cultures to those of Africa, Central and South America, and the South Seas. A permanent exhibit at the **Haffenreffer Museum of Anthropology** (Mount Hope, Bristol, 253-8388) shows some of the highlights of the collections. Changing exhibits study some facet of the vast collections in depth; the current main exhibit examines what museums like this are all about, offering a revealing glimpse into the back rooms and into the collection and research methods. There have been mumblings from Brown for years about moving this museum to Providence (or about burying it forever by absorbing it into the art museums), but we'll believe it when we see the moving trucks.

The museum sits on land that was once the stronghold of the Wampanoags, and not far from the building is a site that has always been associated with King Phillip, their chief. Follow the trail to see **King Phillip's Seat**, a stone ledge that, according to tradition, was used by the Wampanoag leader, best known to history for King Phillip's Wars in the colonial era.

SECRET PADDLES

⚜

If, like me, you feel half-dressed traveling without your kayak on the roof rack, you'll want to know that there are good put-ins at the Elm Street Pier, off Washington Street in The Point; at Third Beach in Middletown (see "Secret Beaches"); and at King's Beach Park on Wellington Avenue, which you can get to from the end of Thames Street. Off season, you can use nearly any of the beaches, but in mid-summer it's tough to carry anything bigger than a sand pail across the hem-to-hem patchwork of beach towels. If you plan to paddle to Rose Island in the spring or early summer, call the Rose Island Lighthouse Foundation (847-4242) to make sure it's not nesting season — or stay 20 yards offshore. It's OK to beach there otherwise. Remember that there is a lot of traffic in and out of the harbor and the bay, and not all of it can stop on a dime, so stay well out of the way of both motorized and sail boats. **Adventure Watersports** (142 Long Wharf, 849-4820) rents kayaks and canoes. **Ocean State Adventures** (99 Poppasquash Road, Bristol, 254-4000) guides kayak trips that focus on local ecosystems.

SECRET PASSAGE
✤

Touro Synagogue (85 Touro Street, 847-4794, see "Secret Judaica") has a secret passage — or at least the end of a filled-in tunnel, directly underneath the point where the rabbi stands. He's actually standing on the trap door over it. No one knows why it's there, where it goes, or what it was used or intended for. Several theories have suggested connections with the Underground Railroad or a quick escape route — but why and for whom, we can only guess. Like the Old Stone Mill (see "Secret Mill"), the synagogue keeps its secrets.

SECRET PETS
✤

Ruling grande dame Mamie Fish once gave a formal dinner party for the pets of the summer set, which caused quite a bit of public criticism, since it was in the middle of an economic slump when many people were out of work. Later, Doris Duke allowed her beloved dogs the run of the house, and kept nets over the finest of the embroidered silk upholstery to protect it from well-manicured paws. When she died, she left a trust fund for the dogs' care, so they could continue to live at Rough Point. You can pamper your pet with all-natural premium dog biscuits from **The Gourmet Dog** (476B

Thames Street, 841-9301). They are low in fat and contain no preservatives. Among the other pet products in this downstairs boutique are cat biscuits, dishes, pillows, and greeting cards.

SECRET PHOTOGRAPHY

⚜

Between gates, foliage, and the direction of the sun, photographing some of Newport's sights can be a challenge. In general, you will get the best photos of the mansions from the Cliff Walk in the morning and from Bellevue Avenue in the afternoon. A morning tour of Rough Point puts the light on the mansion's ocean-facing side, which is the best viewpoint. In the afternoon, you will have to be creative in finding an end angle. The Chinese Teahouse at Marble House is difficult to get face-on, since it faces north, but you can do well with afternoon sun from the side. The Breakers photographs well in afternoon light, since the west side has enough lawn for you to step back and get the whole mansion without a wide-angle lens.

The facades of several of the mansions can be photographed through their fences even when the houses are closed in the off season — Rosecliff has only a low hedge, Beechwood no fence, and Marble House a fence with holes large enough to accommodate a lens. There's also a good view of the front of The Breakers from Cliff Walk.

SECRET PICNICS

⚜

Sandwiches are the forte of **The Market** (43 Memorial Boulevard, 848-2600), and not just the same old combos. The rosemary-scented chicken salad has almonds and the occasional tang of dried apricots, for example. The shop will pack an entire lunch that includes potato salad, fruit, Brie, and dessert.

Locals depend on **Slice of Heaven** (32 Narragansett Avenue, Jamestown, 423-3970) year round. You'll have to line up behind the summer people between June and September if you hope to carry away a panini filled with grilled ham and brie with caramelized onions, or a focaccia chock-full of roasted vegetables and goat cheese, in your picnic basket. Salads are fresh, crisp, and often inspired, and you can finish off with a linzer cookie or a slice of Normandy apple tart. Or you can eat right there, in the sunny cafe, or on picnic tables overlooking a not-very-scenic stretch of Narragansett Avenue.

My favorite place for a quiet picnic with a view is down at The Point, in the **John J. Martins Memorial Park** (Washington Street), where benches overlook Rose Island and the bay. It's even better as the setting sun paints the sky over Jamestown and reflects in the water.

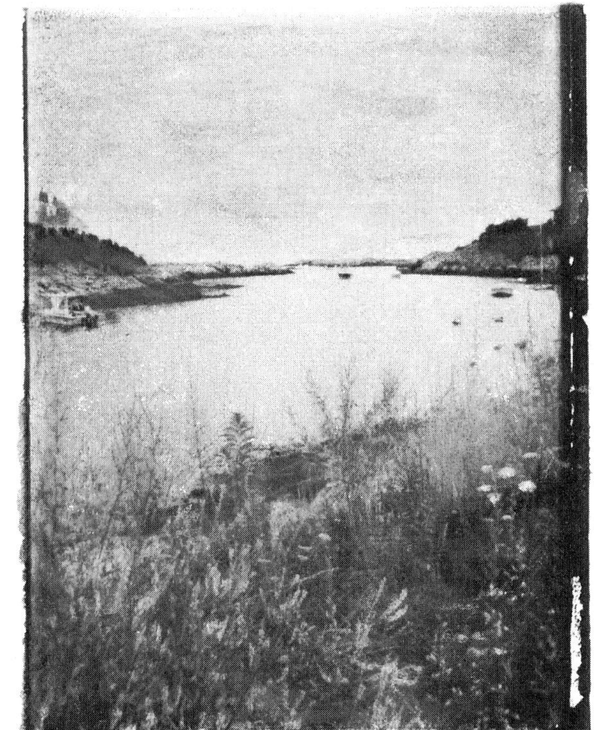

SECRET
PIZZA
✿

At **Via Via** (372 Lower Thames Street, 846-4074), you can choose the topping for your slice of brick-oven pizza from a sophisticated list that includes marinated artichoke hearts and wild mushrooms. Prices are low on pizza slices, or you can order sandwiches or pasta dishes to eat in the small informal dining room. Best part is, you can have pizza for an early breakfast at 6 AM or a late night snack at 2 AM. They never seem to sleep.

Pizza Lucia (186 Thames Street, 847-6355), like its sister restaurant next door, specializes in Bolognese styles, so why not go with the flow and order a fried pizza called a crescentina.

SECRET
PLANTS
✿

In late June or early July, the **Newport Flower Show at Rosecliff** (Bellevue Avenue, 847-1000) includes, along with the usual flower arrangements and displays, a marketplace of horticultural marvels. This is a chance to buy rare plants and hybrids from all over the United States that are available nowhere else. Often grown by private plant breeders whose hobby has become a passion, the plants are for many the highlight of the show. As one eager gardener told me, "It's crammed with goodies."

Historically, Newport gardens were filled with unusual and exotic plants. Varieties were brought home by early ship captains and flourished well north of their usual zone because of Newport's mild winter climate. At the turn of the 20th century, Victorians were fascinated with plant breeding and many of their experiments are still growing in Newport gardens today. The American Beauty rose was first bred at Rosecliff.

SECRET PLAYGROUNDS

❖

If adults turn their heads in astonishment as they pass the giant playground behind the **Jamestown Philomenian Library** (26 North Road, Jamestown, 423-7280), imagine how kids react. Wooden castles to defend, ladders to climb, swings, and slides are all built into as aesthetic a complex as I've ever wanted to play in myself.

Portsmouth Playground has smaller, but similarly well-built, wooden architectural equipment, with towers and plenty of places to climb and pretend. Look for it on Route 24, just south of where it splits from Route 144.

Near Bellevue Avenue in Newport is a nice public playground in **Aquidneck Park**, on Spring Street.

SECRET PAYHOUSE

※

A fire consumed the original estate that **The Breakers** (Ochre Point Avenue at Ruggles Avenue, 847-1000, see "Secret Style") replaced. The only thing that survived is the charming Play House, which sits almost hidden in the landscaped grounds designed by the firm of Frederick Law Olmsted, whose work you will see elsewhere in the Newport area. You'll find it between the house and the side gate. In the summer you can go inside this Queen Anne building, which is the size of a small cottage. Four caryatides support the porch roof, each different. A satyr with pointy ears holds grapes, Vanity admires herself in a mirror, a hunchback plays the pipes, and another hides behind a masque. Inside is a beautiful paneled room with a fireplace.

SECRET POLO

※

From early June to early September, polo ponies perform their intricate maneuvers in the **Newport International Polo Series** (Glen Farm, Route 138, Portsmouth, 846-0200). Matches start at 5 PM on Saturdays. The International Series Grand Prix is played there the last weekend in August; it's fun to watch even if you know nothing about the game.

SECRET
ROOFTOPS

If you cross Thames Street from the **Brick Alley Pub** (140 Thames Street, 849-6334) and look up, you'll see a bright red fire engine poised on the roof of the building. It's not a plastic replica, but the real Engine #4, 1946 vintage, put there after it was given to the owner by friends.

Inside the pub are more wheeled vehicles, including a pickup truck and associated memorabilia, such as license plates. Along the ceiling runs a model train on a suspended track. So if you wake up the next morning after too many pints of ale there, and feel as though a train has run over your head, it did. Trains on the ceiling are not unique to the Brick Alley, however. You'll find another at **Friends Bar and Grill** (32 Broadway, 846-3659), opposite Aiden's.

You'd never guess by looking at **The Elms** (367 Bellevue Avenue, at Dixon Street, 847-1000) that behind the low-appearing balustrade above its second story hide servants' quarters and clotheslines. You can visit these in the unique Behind the Scenes tour (see "Secret Backstairs"), when you can also go to the back of the roof for an excellent bird's eye view of the newly restored sunken garden behind the mansion. There's also a surprising close-up view of the larger-than-life backsides of the nude statues that grace the top corners of the building.

At the other end of Bellevue Avenue, **Beaulieu**, still a private home, was the summer estate of Grace and Cornelius Vanderbilt, Jr. Alice Roosevelt, daughter of President Theodore Roosevelt, scandalized the town when she danced the hootchie-kootchie along its quite visible mansard roof. Unlike the statues at The Elms, she was fully dressed.

SECRET ROYALTY
✤

Newporters seem to have forgiven the Brits all. They welcomed Queen Elizabeth to open the park in front of Trinity Church in celebration of the Bicentennial in 1976. **Trinity Church** (Queen Anne's Square, 846-0660) began life as a Church of England establishment. Queen Anne donated the bell — probably the first one to ring in a New England church — and the communion silver. A gilt lion and unicorn once held the royal arms above the altar, but as soon as the British army left town, a group of patriots destroyed the crest in a public bonfire. They couldn't reach the crown at the top of the steeple. At the far right of the altar are two old prayer books in a glass case; in one of them, all references to the Crown have been crossed out or pasted over.

When Queen Elizabeth came for the Bicentennial, she used the same pew where George Washington had worshiped, now marked by the royal and presidential seals on the needlepoint kneelers. Newport's own "royalty" attended Trinity and, as they thought befitted their station, had their private pews upholstered in colors (perhaps to match the liveries of their household staff). Many also had comfortable easy chairs in place of benches. Pew 66, in pale blue velour, belonged to the Vanderbilts.

The Four Hundred was fascinated by European royalty, with or without a throne, and welcomed the Duke and Duchess of Windsor with open arms. They were often guests at a mansion that is now a B&B, **Elm Tree Cottage** (336 Gibbs Avenue, 849-1610 or 1-800-882-3356). You can sleep in the handsome Windsor Suite where they stayed, with its carved bed, vintage linens, antiques, and spacious silver-set bathroom.

Due to their fascination with royalty, most of Newport's upper crust decorated their homes with royals' portraits or former belongings. The ladies' reception room adjoining the front entrance of The Breakers is lined with carved and gilt paneling commissioned by Marie Antoinette for the Paris home of her godchild. Belcourt Castle has King Charles II's jousting armor, a portrait of Louis XIV that was cut from its frame as the Tuilleries burned during the French Revolution, and a full gold-lined porcelain tea set that was carried into battle by Napoleon.

SECRET SAILING

If you don't know a spinnaker from spinach, you can keep your ignorance a secret by taking a short course in the basics. **Sail Newport** (The Sailing Center, Fort Adams State Park, 849-8385) gives a two-hour sailing sampler tour — a quick course in sailing technique — as well as longer courses. Children from age 7 can learn sailing here. The non-profit organization also rents sailboats and operates sailing tours.

SAILING

SECRET SAILORS

❖

The US Navy and Newport have been close friends since 1775, when the Rhode Island Navy sloop *Katy* defeated the British *Diana* in the first naval battle of the Revolution. In 1884, the Navy founded **The Naval War College** (Gate 1, Naval Education and Training Center, 841-4052 or 841-1317), with a museum that shows the history of the US Navy in Narragansett Bay. In it are good World War II photos, a torpedo collection, and beautiful large-scale ship models. The **Naval Education and Training Center** has pass-in-review ceremonies that are open to the public. It also offers ship tours on weekend afternoons from May to September.

At 141 Pelham Street, at the corner of Bellevue Avenue, the building with the wrap-around porch is the Elks Home. But during the Civil War, the US Naval Academy stood here, in a previous building. Annapolis was perilously near Confederate Virginia, so the Academy sailed north from 1861 to 1865. Midshipmen used to parade in Touro Park, across the street.

SECRET SALVATION

❖

When you've had it up to your highbrow eyebrows with Gilded Age ostentation and you yearn for something real — and real good — the funky decor and inspired fusion menu at **Salvation Café** (140

Broadway, 847-2620) will save your sanity. I head for the most outrageous-sounding dishes — pan-seared chicken that's been marinated in stout, coffee, and vanilla beans — or the more delicately flavored ones, like scallops in an orange and rice-wine broth. I never have room for dessert after the generous servings, but the chocolate mousse looks pretty tempting. Salvation is a good choice for weekend brunch, with such eye-openers as green chili pork hash or portobello mushrooms topped with poached eggs and a chili hollandaise. And although I loathe stuffed French toast, they at least do it stylishly with mascarpone and rum-sodden raisins.

SECRET SCRIMSHAW

It's all legally obtained material, in case the word scrimshaw makes your hair stand on end. **Scrimshanders** (14 Bowen's Wharf, 849-5680 or 1-800-635-5234) creates and sells delicate modern carvings, and hard-to-find antique scrimshaw. Neither is inexpensive, as you would guess. The shop also carries other ivory antiques and Nantucket Lightship baskets, as well as another rare art born of long lonely days at sea — sailors' Valentines.

SECRET
SEAFOOD

❖

Way down Thames, where tourists seldom reach, Newporters head to **The West Deck** (1 Waite's Wharf, 847-3610) for new and creative takes on their favorite fresh local catch. The menu changes frequently, so diners are never bored. I've rarely met a sea bass I didn't like, so perhaps I'm not a fair judge, but The West Deck's was regally robed in Greek olives, an excellent pairing. The terrace bar overlooking the bay attracts locals on summer evenings.

Forever with a twenty-something line trailing off down the street, **Scales & Shells** (527 Thames Street, 846-FISH) doesn't seem to be a secret to anyone. It's always over-crowded, always noisy, and always serves superbly fresh seafood, cooked just right. Everybody knows that the restaurant doesn't take reservations and just comes prepared to stand in line. Here's the secret: the restaurant does take reservations for its second-floor alter ego, **Up Scales**, where the menu's identical — the day's catch, prepared in straightforward ways, best on the mesquite-fired grill that heats one side of the dining room. No credit cards, and it's only open spring through fall.

Don't look for fusion or New American, but do expect inexpensive, fresh, and respectfully prepared fish at **Dry Dock Seafood** (448 Thames Street, at Howard Street, 847-3974). The decor's not much, either, but the grilled sardines are delectable and the fish & chips is never greasy. You'll find the cheapest fisherman's platter in town, and tasty baked stuffed shrimp. No reservations, no wine or beer, and no plastic. But no surprises when the check comes, either.

SECRET SEATS
✤

The biggest problem with a walking town like Newport is that after several hours of strolling, your feet want to stop for a while. And there are not a lot of public benches — or, at least, not many easily visible ones. A block off Bellevue, **Aquidneck Park** (Spring and Bowrey streets) is a large area of lawns with benches. Stone benches line **Cliff Walk**, just south (to the right) of the Narragansett Street entrance at Forty Steps. The **Ann Street Pier** (Lower Thames Street) is shorter than its neighboring piers, with benches at the end, so you can sit and watch the boats go back and forth. **Patriot's Park** (Touro Street) is the pleasant, sunny little garden with benches at Touro Synagogue.

If you're very small, and want a really secret place to sit, find the **Moon Gate** facing onto Shepard Avenue, on the grounds of Chateau-sur-Mer. Narrow stairs lead to the top of this round stone gate, where there is a small stone chair to perch upon.

SECRET SLAVES
✤

Newport's **Long Wharf** was the New England apex in the Triangle Trade in colonial days, when ships arrived with cargoes of molasses from the West Indies to be made into rum, which was shipped to

West Africa to trade for slaves. Slaves arrived with the molasses, and slave ownership was common among Newporters, with most of the town's leading homes staffed by slaves. Southern families traveled here for the summer with their household servants, too, so Blacks were a common sight on Newport streets. Several slave-related sites remain today.

Trinity Church still has slave pews beside the organ, and the **Common Ground** cemetery (Farewell and Warner streets, see "Secret Graves") has America's largest group of tombstones for African-Americans from the period before the Revolution. One is signed "Stevens," one of the best-known early stone carvers. This is especially significant since, elsewhere, slaves were rarely even given a marked grave, let alone a stone someone had to pay a top stonecutter to make. The slave cemetery is right along Farewell Street, near the boundary fence between the Common Ground and Island cemeteries.

The first **free Black church** in America was founded in 1824 by 12 Newporters, who built the Colored Union Church and Society at 49 Division Street. The building soon became a stop on the Underground Railroad. The **Newport Historical Society** (82 Touro Street, 846-0813, see "Secret Ancestors") houses the account books of the Newport slave traders.

SECRET SNOBS

❖

Newport was the summer playground of New York's Four Hundred. The term originated with a comment of Newport summer resident

Ward McAllister, who said there were only 400 people really worth knowing (400 was the capacity of Mrs. Astor's New York ballroom).

You'll know you've made it when you get to dip your toes with the elite at **Bailey's Beach**, near the southern end of Bellevue Avenue. It's the private and almost sacrosanct preserve of Newport society, and you need an invitation to so much as set foot there. It's not the best beach — it's the cachet that counts. Mrs. Belmont of Belcourt Castle swam at Bailey's shaded by a green parasol, and as a child Doris Duke won a trophy in a sandcastle competition here.

To see some modern-day snobbery at work, just hang around the mansions for a while. Following the old tradition of the hired help taking on the airs and affectations of their employers, some of the haughtiest and least hospitable people in Newport may greet you from behind the ticket desks of The Breakers or The Elms. You may also find some of the nicest people there, so this is certainly not the rule, as it was in the Gilded Age. And, that said, let me add that the guides in the Preservation Society properties and other sites are usually top notch, well informed, and able to spin a good tale.

SECRET SOCKS

At the end of America's Cup Avenue, where it meets Memorial Boulevard and Thames Street, is one of my favorite public artworks. Where the sidewalk curves around Perry's Mill, there rises from the sidewalk the graceful curve of a five-foot ocean wave. From "The Wave" extend two feet, grown shiny from the hands that touch them in passing. In cold weather they are often warmly covered in socks. "The Wave" is the work of Kay Worden, but whose work the socks are is unknown. Sometimes the socks match, more often they don't. I've never actually seen anyone changing the footwear, but they are usually different each time I go by.

SECRET STATUARY

Second only to the decorations in their "cottages" was the ornamentation in the gardens of the Four Hundred and the Four Hundred wannabes. You'll see statues imitating everything from ancient Greece and Rome artworks to Japanese stone lanterns. Fountains aren't just fountains: water springs out of everything from grotesque masques to the mouths of dolphins.

As lesser mansions bit the dust, it was inevitable that some of these bits of outdoor stonework would end up in the things-too-big-to-get-rid-of category. Fortunately, **The Aardvark** (2 J.T. Connell Highway, 849-7233, www.aardvarkantiques.com) is there to rescue them. As you drive into Newport from the bridge, you'll see its yard full of Greek goddesses, Corinthian columns, stylized fish, and a plethora of other stone frufru. The shop inside carries antiques and other previously owned funky stuff.

SECRET STYLE
✥

If you are interested in interior decoration and in the evolution of its styles, **The Breakers** (Ochre Point Avenue at Ruggles Avenue, 847-1000) is a textbook. It was here that the innovative decorator Ogden Codman revolutionized American decorative style by eschewing the heavy dark woods and overstuffed furniture beloved of the Victorians. Instead, the 30-year-old Bostonian used light colors for the walls, woodwork, and furniture. Windows are large to let in the light and are actually allowed to do so — almost a heresy to the Victorian eye. Codman did not shun heavy and ornate decoration, but his intricate cornices (note especially those in the second-floor guest room) are clearly visible in their paler colors and with ample light.

Even when Codman used darker colors, as he did in the library on the first floor, the effect is elegant without being either somber or heavy. The deeply coffered ceiling uses a dolphin motif highlighted with 24-karat gold. The entire room — walls, ceiling, and bookcases — are all done in decorated paneling. To me, this is the most stunning room in the house. The music room, which was designed and built in Paris, has hand-carved wood paneling, about half of which is covered in 22-karat gold. This and the adjoining morning room are the two chambers most like the palaces of Europe, with almost every inch covered in decoration of some sort. For its size and surfeit of decoration, the prize goes to the formal dining room, with its dozen rose marble columns soaring toward the ceiling 50 feet above. From it hang the two largest Baccarat chandeliers in existence.

Codman's *The Decoration of Houses*, which he co-authored with Edith Wharton, became the bible of interior decoration.

SECRET
SURF
✥

The low lay of the land and the open water surrounding it makes Newport a prime place for surfing. Surf's most likely to be up at **Fort Adams State Park**, and at **Second Beach** (the best) and **Third Beach**, both in Middletown. At the latter two, south or southeast onshore winds bring long rolling breakers. **Easton's Beach** (Memorial Boulevard) and **Second Beach** have designated surfing areas. Tune to 95.5 FM at 8:35 each morning to hear where the tide's up.

Water Brothers Surf and Sport (39 Memorial Boulevard, 849-4990) rents boards and suits, and offers three-day surfing classes three days weekly in July, when the water cooperates. Water Brothers also has a good line of other sports clothing and equipment, including snowboards, skateboards, and inline skates.

Island Sports (86 Aquidneck Avenue, near Easton's Beach, 846-4421) offers lessons (with a simulator) and rentals of windsurfing and surfing equipment, from its summer location on Third Beach and from the shop.

SECRET
SURPLUS
✥

Where they get it, I don't know, but there's a never-ending supply of GI clothing, outdoor gear, and foul weather clothing at the **Army Navy Store** (262 Thames Street, 847-3073), one of the few of its genre left. Newport's been awash with military for at least a century, and I suspect this place began as a sort of thrift shop for all those things sailors and soldiers used to be so good at liberating from government jurisdiction. Anyway, it's the real thing, and dates to before World War II. Rather than just nostalgia items and costumes, look for good camping gear, leather flight jackets, Eastern European military wear, high-tech sunglasses and binocs, and just good sturdy clothes.

SECRET SWEETS

Not just any sweets — they're chocolate. **Newport Chocolates** (82 William Street, 841-8975) makes enough varieties — pushing 100 — to keep anybody in a state of chocolate euphoria. My favorites are the champagne truffles, but I've always had expensive tastes. The collection of molds isn't limited to Easter bunnies and fat Santas, so if you need a gift for a sailing friend, consider ordering a chocolate sailboat.

SECRET TEA

Nobody outdid Alva Vanderbilt when it came to tea houses, and her bright red **Chinese Tea House** at Marble House (Bellevue Avenue, 847-1000) is the undisputed champion. It used to be about 75 feet closer to the sea, but the cliffs began to deteriorate — and eventually fell into the sea — so it was moved. When Alva (by this time she was Mrs. Belmont, mistress of Belcourt Castle) introduced it at a ball in 1914, it was illuminated in lantern light, and approached along a lantern-lit pathway over a Chinese bridge. More discreetly, the two small tea houses at **The Elms** (Bellevue Avenue, at Dixon Street, 847-1000) flank the entrance to a formal sunken garden with patterned boxwood hedges.

You can enjoy a relaxing afternoon tea yourself at Newport's bastion of Brit, **Elizabeth's** (404 Lower Thames Street, 846-6862), where it's properly steeped and served in china pots. All the proper accompaniments are there: tender cream scones, fancy tea cakes, buttery little tea biscuits that melt on your tongue, thin tea sandwiches, and a selection of "savories."

Notable afternoon tea is also served to the public at **Vanderbilt Hall** (41 Mary Street, 846-6200 or 1-888-VANHALL, www.vanderbilthall.com) and to guests at both the **Cliffside Inn** (see "Secret Artist") and the **Adele Turner Inn** (see "Secret Breakfasts"), where the tea is poured into a collection of fine china cups and saucers.

SECRET
TENNIS

When **The Casino** (194 Bellevue Avenue, 849-3990) was built in 1880, it was America's most complete sports facility, with racquet courts, croquet lawns, a bowling alley, a theater, shops, and a cafe. Lawn tennis was a new sport in the States, and it got its start here. Of

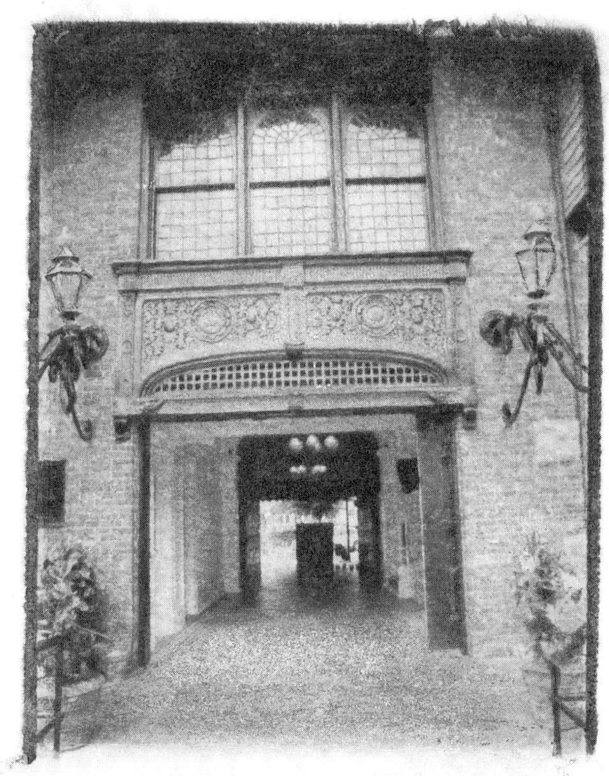

course, it was a private facility then, but now you can reserve grass court time or try "court tennis," the 13th-century forerunner to the modern game.

The **International Tennis Hall of Fame** is in the same building, with exhibits — some of them interactive — on tennis and its greats. Tennis tournaments are nearly always going on, and you can watch free from the benches, or from the cafe on the balcony.

If you don't think your game is up to such public scrutiny, go to the public courts a couple of blocks away at **Aquidneck Park**, next to the Senior Center, which are free and don't have spectator benches.

SECRET
TIKI BAR
✢

Remember those? The outdoor bars under thatched roofs, where you whiled away summer evenings at the beach? There's one hidden behind the **Salvation Café** (140 Broadway, 847-2620), as crowded and noisy as the ones right on the sand. You can get all exotic with tropical rum drinks, or drink plain old beer. Sorry, no limbo dancing.

SECRET
TOURS
✢

Of course, you can climb onto a bus and ride through Newport for an overview and some funny guide-stories, but the best way to meet

Newport is on foot. More specifically with Anita Raphael, of **Newport on Foot** (846-5391). Anita's understanding of the city's past has no rival. She goes far beyond the chronological facts to share insights and anecdotes that bring 10 blocks of colonial Newport to life. Anita also escorts tours on specialized subjects, such as Newport cabinetmakers, craftsmen, and taverns, and she offers a ghost and graveyard tour at Halloween. Reservations are essential for the theme tours and are suggested for any of them.

SECRET TRANSPORT

Most visitors pay $5 to climb aboard the trolley, but in the summer a free shuttle bus covers the most popular tourist routes every half hour on weekdays and every 20 minutes on weekends. Not only is it free, but on weekends it also runs a little more frequently than the trolley.

You can make a trip to beautiful Block Island from Newport, via the **Block Island Ferry**, operated by the Interstate Navigation Company (783-4613). It leaves daily in the summer, at 10:30 AM, from Fort Adams State Park.

Instead of driving across the bridge to Jamestown, you can ride the **Jamestown and Newport Ferry** (423-9900), which leaves from Goat Island and drops you right in the heart of Jamestown. For another dollar you can take your bike to the island, which is fairly level and easily explored on two wheels.

Rhode Island Public Transit Authority (RIPTA) buses connect Newport to Providence. They leave each city at least once an hour on weekdays, every two hours on weekends. All buses arrive in Newport at the transportation center, which adjoins the visitors' center. Taxis, very pricey in Newport, wait just outside. RIPTA also operates buses within Newport, so if you are arriving by bus, ask your hosts before you arrive whether they are close to one of RIPTA's lines. RIPTA fares are very, very cheap.

SECRET TREASURE
✣

If I could tell you exactly where to find this, I'd be writing this book from my desk in that lovely little sitting room off the landing at Marble House, ringing for one of the staff to bring me a tea tray. But local legend holds that Captain Kidd's Treasure Cave, where his cache was reputed to have been hidden, is in or about what is now **Fort Wetherill State Park** (East Shore Road, Jamestown, 423-9941 in summer or 884-2010 year round, see "Secret Forts"). Of course, I have heard the same said of just about every other rocky point from Newfoundland to the Carolinas, but I'm just passing on what I've been told. Jamestown does have a pretty solid connection with the pirate, since he was a friend of the local privateer, Captain Thomas Paine. This much is historically founded. Just how closely Paine was associated with Kidd was the subject of an investigation when Kidd was finally captured.

SECRET
TREES
✤

If grandly spreading trees from exotic climes make your heart beat faster, you need a copy of ***Newport Landscapes***, published by the Preservation Society of Newport County. This virtually unknown guide has the landscaping plans of all the mansions and other properties owned by the society. It identifies each of the significant trees by location and includes leaf silhouettes to help you identify them. The text fills in some interesting history and anecdotes about the origins of trees, the garden designers, and some of the outdoor parties these trees have witnessed.

Exotic trees grew in Newport long before the gardeners of the Gilded Age tended them on mansion grounds. This was a sea trade town, and the captains of old brought back citrus and other tropicals, and — lo! — they grew and even flourished on the mild, sea-warmed tip of the island. Victorian Americans, being an inquisitive and excitable lot, were mightily thrilled about horticulture, so they traded trees with their English counterparts and imported yet more spindly twigs from places like Asia and the South Pacific. These, too, survived. So the gracious spreading trees you see today represent a long social history, as well as a horticultural one. And you thought they were just pretty.

Possibly the most photographed tree in town is the Camperdown elm near the Chinese Tea House at **Marble House**, with its elegant spread and twisted limbs. It makes such a good foreground for the long sweeping shot of the mansions along Cliff Walk, and accompaniment for closer shots of the tea house. **Chateau-sur-Mer** has a giant

London plane tree on its Bellevue Avenue lawn and an astonishing European weeping beech near its porte-cochere that forms a room under its drooping branches. **The Elms** has several different varieties of beeches, including copper and fernleaf, as well as a Turkish oak. With the book, you can find them all.

SECRET
VEAL

Although the family's name is synonymous with really good pasta in this area — they have a pasta "factory" in Tiverton — I think the real secret of **Puerini's** (24 Memorial Boulevard, 847-5506) is the veal. While I'm deciding which way I'll ask them to prepare it tonight, I wake up my taste buds with a cherry pepper filled with prosciutto and provolone, nicely seasoned and slightly crisp. Then I make the tough decisions. Veal zingarelle pairs thin slices with roasted red peppers and artichokes, but the veal piccata has a choice of several accompaniments, including sun-dried tomatoes, and is more delicately flavored — not so lemony — than most. Amiable, helpful service may include (as it did the last time I was were there) some very good advice about driving on the Ligurian coast of Italy. The wine list is well priced and includes some very good Italian choices.

SECRET VILLAGE

✣

How can an entire little Swiss village of stone houses — and an arched bridge you could drive a car over — hide so secretively that even many Newporters don't know it's there? Its builder cleverly hid it in a tiny hollow in the rolling landscape of his estate, so only part of it is visible from the top of a rise on Ocean Drive (Ridge Road), about 0.3 miles from the Wellington Avenue intersection. You must be headed toward Wellington Avenue to see it, off to the right.

The village is a "folly," common on the great English baronial estates, but quite rare in America. Follies (Mrs. Vanderbilt's Chinese Tea House is a good example) were built for no practical purpose, often replicating some ancient ruin or exotic structure, just to amuse the owner and his guests. This one was created by the owner of a nearby mansion, who generously invited locals to drive through and admire it on Sunday afternoons. Built from 1914 to 1916, it sought to replicate an Swiss alpine village with its 50 buildings, including houses, outbuildings, stables, a pigsty, and a humpback bridge.

SECRET VINTAGE BOATS

✣

Several brokers represent boats of all types available for charter. One of the best selections is brokered by the **Newport Yacht Charter Association** (1-800-291-5803, www.newportcharters.com), which includes one of my favorite boats in Rhode Island waters, the *Brandaris*. This little converted Dutch *botter* from the Zuider Zee comes with its own World War II history, as one of the many small boats used in the evacuation of Dunkerque. Other boats range from a 155-foot schooner and the 130-foot sloop *Endeavor*, to a 60-foot racing sloop and a 60-foot rumrunner motor yacht from the Roaring '20s. You can entertain your friends on a private cruise or have a party dockside.

SECRET
VIVE LA FRANCE
❧

Remember that it was a French general, Rochambeau, who liberated Newport from the British occupation during the Revolution, so the French have always been close to the hearts of Newporters. A statue in King's Park honors the general, who met in Newport with George Washington to help plan the strategies of the war.

Strictly for its cachet, not for its local historical associations, France seemed to be the favorite motif for Newport society's mansions. Using a little imagination, you can make a quick tour of several "French" landmarks in quick succession. The truest copy is perhaps **The Elms** (Bellevue Avenue, at Dixon Street, 847-1000, see "Secret Backstairs"), which is an almost exact replica of Chateau d'Asnieres. It had everything that palace had, but with modern facilities worked cleverly into the plan. Thousands of tiny details were replicated, from light fixtures to door brasses, most of them custom made. Berwin coal fueled the Vanderbilt railroads, as well as the United States Navy, so Edward Berwin had plenty to spend on the house.

Marble House (Bellevue Avenue, 847-1000) echoes the Petit Trianon at Versailles, and its ballroom was inspired by Versailles' Hall of Mirrors, an eye-boggling room almost entirely awash in gold. Symbols of Louis XIV, the Sun King — sunburst masks of Apollo — decorate the walls, and huge gold chandeliers drop from a ceiling encrusted in gold. The dining room reproduces a salon at Versailles almost exactly.

For a taste of French country style, visit **Rue de France** (78 Thames Street, 846-3636), the only retail store of the high-end catalog distributor that's so important in today's decorating scene. The company is the prime US source of French lace, which you can see and buy in this small boutique. It's not a factory outlet, so you'll pay full price for first-quality merchandise. Stop at the visitors' center and pick up the store's card from the rack; it has a discount coupon attached.

SECRET WHEELS

Aquidneck Island, of which Newport forms the southern end, offers some very good bicycling, with relatively few hills. Ocean Drive, which circles the southern end of the island, is a beautiful route with sea views and splendid mansions (which you can't stop to admire nearly so easily in a car). Take a spin down almost any street off Bellevue to see more mansions and fine homes, whose yards are often shaded by exotic trees. From a bike you can stop to admire the well-kept gardens. Remember, however, that many streets are one-way, which applies to bicycles, too.

The visitors' center has a very good brochure entitled ***A Bicyclist's Guide to Aquidneck Island***, with maps of the island and Newport's streets. It shows the hills (blessedly few), as well as those areas and streets with particularly heavy traffic. Useful details, such as the fact that you can't ride a bike over the Newport Bridge, are included.

Ten Speed Spokes (18 Elm Street, at the corner of America's Cup Avenue, next to the visitors' center, 847-5609) rents all-new road and mountain bicycles by the hour, day, or week. Cycling maps, helmets, and locks are included. Staff there can repair your own bike, too. **Newport Wheels** (Unit 2, Brown and Howard Wharf, off Thames Street, 849-4400) rents mountain bikes.

SECRET
WINDMILL
❖

Windmills were very useful in early Newport history, for the same reason that Newport is a great place to fly kites: there's usually a steady breeze. Only two windmills remain, one a familiar sight to people driving down Route 114 to Newport. But I think the 1787 **Jamestown Windmill** (North Road, off Route 138, Jamestown, 423-1798) is the most fun to visit. Thanks to a recent restoration, you can go up into the top floor to see how a windmill works, using big cog wheels and a dome that turns so the huge wooden arms can face the wind. The windmill at **Prescott Farm** (2009 West Main Road [Route 114], Middletown, 849-7300) dates from 1812 and still grinds Rhode Island flint corn — the kind you need to make jonnycakes (see "Secret Jonnycakes").

SECRET YACHTS

Even if you don't have a yacht that needs repair, you can stop in at the **International Yacht Restoration School** (449 Thames Street, 848-5777, www.iyrs.org) just to look at the boats. And if you want to learn the fine art of boat restoration, there's no better place. Classes include tool sharpening, steel bending, machinery, lofting, refinishing, planking, and yacht surveying (the important skill of being able to tell whether there's enough left of a boat to restore). A spring Tuesday evening lecture series explores different aspects of wooden boat work.

SECRET FUTURE

No guidebook can even pretend to be comprehensive, especially when the objective is to unearth hidden places and previously unheard-of events. Without a doubt, some worthwhile attractions have resisted our attempts to dig them up.

In the interest of improving future editions of this book, please let us know about the sites, sounds, and tastes you've discovered that warrant inclusion. If we use your suggestion, we'll send you a free copy on publication. Please contact us at the following address:

Secret Providence and Newport
c/o ECW PRESS

2120 Queen Street East, Suite 200
Toronto, Ontario, Canada M4E 1E2

Or e-mail us at: info@secretguides.com

PHOTO SITES

FRONT COVER:
BACK COVER: near Spring Street, Newport

SECRET PROVIDENCE

Page	
22	Wickenden Street
26	First Unitarian Church, Benefit Street
38	Hope Street
41	Pole Art, Wickendon Street
54	Roger Williams Park
60	off Benefit Street
73	Brown University
78	River
85	Culinary Museum
89	State House
91	Athanaeum
104	River Boardwalk
100	Providence Theatre
114	Waterplace
116	Athanaeum
120	New York System, Plainville Street

SECRET NEWPORT

Page	
130	Tuoro Park
142	Baseball stadium
152	"Tatters"
157	Linden Place
169	Chateau-sur-Mer
174	Mary Street
182	Tuoro Synagogue
194	Topiary Museum
202	Ocean Drive
209	Goat Island Lighthouse
221	Tennis Hall of Fame

SUBJECT INDEX

Providence

Accommodations
Old Court, The 117
Providence Biltmore 117
Samuel Slater Canal Boat 48
State House Inn 25

Adult Fun
Foxy Lady Club 68
Ethnic Concepts 100
Sportsman's Inn 58
Miko Exoticware 66

Architecture and Buildings
See also Sacred and Hallowed Places
City Hall 90
Corliss-Bracket House 72
Downcity 45
Festival of Historic Houses 59
First Baptist Meeting House 25
Governor Henry Lippett House 115
Greenwich Odeum 109
Luminaria Candlelight Tour 61
Providence Preservation Society 57
Providence Performing Arts Center 109
Providence Art Club 51
Roger Williams Park Casino 118
St. Stephen's Church 57
State House 43
Woods Gerry Mansion 72

Bakeries
Kaplan's Bakery 36
Pastiche 106
Scialo Bros. Bakery 105

Bargains and Freebies
See also Vintage and Antiques
John Brown House 21
Lorraine Mill Fabics 98
New Rivers 119
Ocean State Job Lot 82
Ryco Factory Outlet 98
Slater Factory Fabrics 98
Textile Warehouse 99
Tinsel Town and Patioland 35
Water Ferry 40
Yarn Outlet, The 98

Bars, Booze, and Wine
See also Nightlife
Cafe Paragon 101
Diamond Hill Vineyards 118

Books and Literary Interests
John Hay Library 90
Myopic Books 29
Providence Athenaeum 45
RI Historical Society Library 47
Swan Point Cemetery 61
Union Saint-Jean Baptiste D'Amerique 50

Child's Play
Crescent Park Carousel 31
Dalrymple Boathouse 58
India Point Park 83
Slater Loof Carousel 31

Coffee and Tea
See also Sweets
Coffee Exchange 37
Indigo Herbals 122
L'Elizabeth 108
Market House 108

Ethnic Eating
See also Restaurants
Angelo's Civita Farnese 74
Aspara 70
Bocce Club 33
Cafe Yuni 71
Caffe Itri 65
Chan's 34
Friends Market 87
L'Osteria 65
L'Epicurio 64
Lisboa a Noite 88
Mayor's Own Marinara Sauce 74

Pakarang 108
Pasta Challenge 86
Prairie Diner 102
Ran Zan 105
Roberto's Diner 82
Seaplane Diner 102
Serra d'Estrella 88
Taste of India 96
Valley Park Cervezeria 87
Venda Ravioli 64

Fashion, Clothing, and Accessories
BEDLAM! 42
Copacetic Rudely Elegant Jewelry 69
Miko Exoticware 66

Fast Food/To Go
Iggy's Doughboys 44
Olneyville New York System 119
Spoons 102

Fairs and Festivals
Bastille Day Restaurant Race 27
Cape Verdian Independence Day 88
Chinese New Year 33
Clown 39
Federal Hill 64
Heritage Day 45
International Holiday Sale 34
Jubilee Franco Americain 50
Pasta Challenge 86
RI Labor and Ethnic Heritage Festival 67
WaterFire 28

Film and Video
Cable Car Cinema 35

Flora and Fauna
See also Parks and Gardens
Brown University Conservatory 65
Charles H. Smith Greenhouse 121
Llama Farma, The 69
Lime Rock Preserve 121
Mounted Command Building 59
Roger Williams Park Zoo 96
Sabin Point Parrots 84

Furniture and Home Design
Helianthus 51
Textile Warehouse 99
Tinsel Town and Patioland 35

Gay and Lesbian
Castro, The 55

Grocers and Food Shops
See also Fast Food/To Go; Sweets
Arcade, The 99
Friends Market 87
Goodie Basket, The 56
Venda Ravioli 64

Health and Beauty
See also Recreation and Fitness
Hair-2-E-tan-ity 47
Hairspray 40
Public Restrooms 76

History and Heritage
See also Museums, Galleries, Historic Homes
Heritage Day 45
Langston Hughes Center 28
RI Historical Society Library 47
RI Labor and Ethnic Heritage Festival 67
RI Black Heritage Society 28
Slater Mill 93
Union Saint-Jean Baptiste D'Amerique 50
Valley Falls Park 94

Live Music Venues
See also Nightlife; Performance and Theater
Blackstone River Theatre 49
Castro, The 55
Chan's 34
Lupo's Heartbreak Hotel 76
Met Cafe 77
Pendragon 48

Lunch and Light Meals
See also Fast Food/To Go; Restaurants
Brickway On Wickenden 30
Castro, The 55
Loui's 100
Olneyville New York System 119
Prairie Diner 102
Ran Zan 105
Roberto's Diner 82
Rue de l'Espoir 30
Seaplane Diner 102
Spoons 102
Ye Olde English Fish & Chips 48

Museums, Galleries, Historic Homes
See also History and Heritage
Annmary Brown Memorial 108
AS220 51
Center City Artisans 51
David Winton Bell Gallery 24
Gallery Night 23
Governor Henry Lippett House 115
Helianthus 51
John Hay Library 107
John Brown House 21
Johnson and Wales Culinary Museum 92
Museum of Natural History 42
Providence Art Club 51
RI Watercolor Society 24
RI School of Design Museum 112
Sahah Doyle Gallery 51
Slater Mill 67
Stephen Hopkins House 53

Music Stores
Round Again Records 32

Nightlife
See also Bars, Booze, and Wine; Live Music Venues; Performance and Theater
Foxy Lady Club 68
Lupo's Heartbreak Hotel 76

Parks and Gardens
See also Flora and Fauna; Recreation and Fitness
Blackstone River Valley Nat'l Heritage Corridor 111
Blackstone River State Park 80
Goddard Memorial State Park 27
India Point Park 83
Lincoln Woods State Park 111
Roger Williams Park 80
Shakespeare's Head 53
Stephen Hopkins House 53
Truman Beckwith House 53
Waterplace Park 103

People
Mayor's Own Marinara Sauce (Buddy Cianci) 74
Providence Athenaeum (Poe and Lovecraft) 45
Swan Point Cemetery (Lovecraft) 61

Performance and Theater
See also Live Music Venues
Blackstone River Theatre 49
Blackstone Valley Heritage Concerts 51
Brown University Jazz Band 50
Greenwich Odeum 109
Latin Christmas Carols 35
Leeds Theater 77
NewGate Theatre 77
Perishable Theater 77
Providence Performing Arts Center 109
Providence Early Music Ensemble 50
Stuart Theater 77
Trinity Repertory Company 93
Veteran's Memorial Auditorium 77

Recreation and Fitness
See also Parks and Gardens
Benefit Street 21
Blackstone River State Park 80
Blackstone Blvd 21
Bowling Academy 105
Cranston Country Club 56
Dalrymple Boathouse 58
Down Under Duckpin Bowling 103
Dudek Bowling Alleys 103
East Bay Bike Path 80
Esta's Too 80
Fleet Skating Center 63
Friends of the Blackstone 79
Llama Farma, The 69
Paddle Providence 79
Paddle Sports, Providence 79
Roger Williams Park 80
Sliver Spring Golf Course 56
Sunset Stables 59
Tennis Rhode Island 37
Todd Marsilli Tennis Center 36
Triggs Memorial Golf Course 56
Waterplace Park 21

Resources and Reference
Providence Preservation Society 57
RI Historical Society Library 47
RI Black Heritage Society 28
Union Saint-Jean Baptiste D'Amerique 50

Restaurants
See also Ethnic Eating; Lunch and Light Meals; Vegetarian Havens
3 Steeple Street 31

Angelo's Civita Farnese 74
Aspara 70
Bocce Club 33
Brickway On Wickenden 30
Cafe Yuni 71
Caffe Itri 65
Castro, The 55
Chan's 34
Empire 49
Garden Grille 113
Hemenway's 75
L'Osteria 65
L'Epicurio 64
Lisboa a Noite 88
Loui's 100
New Rivers 119
Pakarang 108
Rachel's Pastanova 86
Ran Zan 105
Roberto's Diner 82
Rue de l'Espoir 30
Serra d'Estrella 88
Taste of India 96
Valley Park Cervezeria 87
Ye Olde English Fish & Chips 48

Sacred and Hallowed Places

Beneficent Congregational Church 33
First Baptist Meeting House 25
Providence Zen Center 81
St. Stephen's Church 57
Swan Point Cemetery 61

Specialty Shops

See also Books and Literary Interests; Fashion, Clothing, and Accessories; Furniture and Home Design; Music Stores; Vintage and Antiques
Copacetic Rudely Elegant Jewelry 69
Ethnic Concepts 100
Goodie Basket, The 56
Indigo Herbals 122
Your Move Games 52

Sports

See also Recreation and Fitness
Pawtucket Red Sox 86

Statues and Public Art

See also Architecture and Buildings
Prospect Park 88

Sweets

See also Coffee and Tea
Coffee Exchange 37
Goodie Basket, The 56
Kaplan's Bakery 36
Maximillian's Ice Cream 63
Pastiche 106
Scialo Bros. Bakery 105

Tours and Trains

Blackstone Valley Explorer 95
Fall Foliage Train Excursion 68
Festival of Historic Houses 59
La Gondola 115
Luminaria Candlelight Tour 61
Providence Transport 112
Self Drive Foliage Tour 68
Water Ferry 40
Water Cruises 42

Trails

Blackstone River Valley National Heritage Corridor 111
Lincoln Woods State Park 111
The Monastery 75

Vegetarian Havens

Aspara 70
Garden Grille 11
Taste of India 96

Views

Prospect Park 88, 117
Providence Biltmore 117

Vintage and Antiques

John Brown House 21
RI School of Design Museum 112
This & That Shop 24
Tilden-Thurber Co. 113
What Cheer! 94

Waterfront

Blackstone Valley Explorer 95
Goddard Memorial State Park 27
India Point Park 83
La Gondola 115
Paddle Providence 79
Water Cruises 42

Newport

Accommodations
Adele Turner Inn 146, 220
Bay Voyage 184
Cliffeside Inn 125, 135, 220
Elm Tree Cottage 208
Francis Malbone House 173
Ivy Lodge 192
Melville Pond Campground 147
Nathaniel Porter Inn 196
Rose Island Lighthouse 126, 138
Vanderbilt Hall 220
Victorian Ladies, The 168

Architecture and Buildings
See also Sacred and Hallowed Places
Belcourt Castle 136
Breakers, The 148, 205, 217
Channing Memorial Church 153
Chateau-sur-Mer 177
Chinese Tea House 219
Edward King House 166
Elms Tea House, The 220
Elms, The 228
Francis Malbone House 173
Hunter House 156
Jamestown Wind Mill 230
Joshua & Co. 148
Kingscote 187
Marble House 229
Newport Congregational Church 153
Ochre Court 166
Old Stone Mill 189
Point, The 156
Prescott Farm 230
Preservation Society of Newport County 165
Redwood Library 133
Rosecliff 147
Rough Point 188
St. Columba Chapel 149
Swiss Village 227

Bargains and Freebies
See also Vintage and Antiques
Edward King House 166
Green Galley, The 150
Lilly's of the Alley 160
Newport Deals 159
Ochre Court 166
Patriots' Shop 160
Preservation Society of Newport County 165

Bars, Booze, and Wine
See also Nightlife
Aiden's Pub 176
Annex, The 132
Brick Alley Pub 206
Newport Blues Cafe 179
Prohibition 175
Salvation Cafe 222
White Lady 128

Books and Literary Interests
Armchair Sailor, The 144
Breakers, The 145
Newport Art Museum 144
Redwood Library 133
Scribe's Perch Bookstore, The 144

Child's Play
Breakers, The 205
Newport Playgrounds 204
Newport Attractions for Kids 183
Newport Kite Festival 186
Sail Newport 208

Coffee and Tea
See also Sweets
Adele Turner Inn 220
Cappuccino's 146, 156
Cheeky Monkey 156
Cliffside Inn 220
Elizabeth's 220
Espresso Yourself Cafe 156
Puerini's 156
Tea & Herb Essence 133
Vanderbilt Hall 220

Ethnic Eating
See also Restaurants
Aiden's Pub 176
Festa Italiana 178
Hisae's 179
Jonnycakes 181
Las Petite Auberge 127
Lucia 177
May Breakfast 181

Nikolas Pizza 173
Puerini's 226
Sea Shai 179
St. Spyridon's Greek Orthodox Church 173

Fashion, Clothing, and Accessories
Army Navy Store 218
Cadeaux du Monde 162
Euphoria! 180
Griffon Shop, The 180
J. H. Breakell, Silversmith 180
Lilly's of the Alley 160
Patriots' Shop 160
Scrimshanders 211
Tatters 151

Fast Food / To Go
Flo's Drive-in 167
Market, The 201
Slice of Heaven 201

Fairs and Festivals
Black Ships Festival 178
Chowder Cook-off 151
Festa Italiana 178
Haunted Newport 137
Irish Music Festival 177
Irish Heritage Month 176
Newport Kite Festival 186
Newport Jazz Festival 179
St. Patrick's Day Parade 176
Weekend of Coaching 155
Newport Flower Show 203

Film and Video
Annex, The 132
Ivy Lodge 192
Jane Pickens Theater 192
Movies Filmed in Newport 191

Flora and Fauna
See also Parks and Gardens
Beavertail State Park 144
Chateau sur Mer 225
Coanicut Island Sanctuary 143
Elms, The 225
Green Animals 132
Marble House 225
Newport Aquarium 161
Newport Flower Show 203
Newport Trees 225

Norman Bird Sanctuary 143
Rose Island 144
Sachuest National Wildlife Refuge 143
Tropical Fish 161

Furniture and Home Design
Aardvark, The 216
Cadeaux du Monde 162
Isle de France 229
Runcible Spoon 185
Thames Glass 171

Grocers and Food Shops
See also Fast Food/To Go; Sweets
Aquidneck Lobster 186

Health and Beauty
See also Recreation and Fitness
Accessible Newport 125
Indigo Herbals 122
Public Restrooms Newport 195
Seaman's Church Institute 125
Tea & Herb Essence 133

History and Heritage
See also Museums, Galleries, Historic Homes
Artillery Company of Newport 134
Beavertail State Park 165
Black History 213
Brenton Point State Park 163
Butts Hill Fort 164
Clifton Burial Ground 172
Common Ground Cemetery 171, 183, 214
Fort Hamilton 164
Fort Wetherill 165
Forty Steps 175
Island Cemetery 172
Jamestown Wind Mill 230
King Phillip's Seat 198
Long Wharf 213
Museum of Newport History 163
Newport Historical Society 131
Old Stone Mill 189
Point, The 156
Prescott Farm 230
Prohibition 175
Rose Island Lighthouse 126
Samuel Whithorne House 193
Trinity Church 172, 207, 214
Whitehorse Tavern 137

Lessons
Yacht Restoration School 231

Live Music Venues
See also Nightlife; Performance and Theater
Aiden's Pub 176
Newport Jazz Venues 180
Red Parrot, The 162, 180

Lunch and Light Meals
See also Fast Food/To Go; Restaurants
Aiden's Pub 176
Brick Alley Pub 206
Cappuccino's 146
Flo's Drive-in 167
Franklin Spa 145
Green Galley, The 150
Hisae's 179
Market, The 201
Mudville's Pub 141
Newport Creamery 138
Nikolas Pizza 173
Pineapple Grill, The 196
Pizza Lucia 203
Quito's 158
Slice of Heaven 201
Via Via 203

Museums, Galleries, Historic Homes
See also History and Heritage
America's Cup Hall of Fame 129
Artillery Company of Newport 134
Belcourt Castle 136
Breakers, The 148, 185, 217
Breakers Stable, The 155
Casino, The 220
Chateau-sur-Mer 177
Elms, The 140, 206
Green Animals 195
Haffenreffer Museum of Anthropology 197
Herreshoff Marine Museum 129
Hunter House 156
Kingscote 187
Mrs Astor's Beechwood 193
Museum of Newport History 163, 184
Naval War College 210
Newport Art Museum 144
Redwood Library 133
Rosecliff 147
Rough Point 188
Samuel Whithorne House 193
Sydney L. Wright Museum 195
Tennis Hall of Fame 222
Wanton-Lyman-Hazard House 168

Nightlife
See also Bars, Booze, and Wine; Live Music Venues; Performance and Theater
Newport Blues Cafe 179

Parks and Gardens
See also Flora and Fauna; Recreation and Fitness
Aquidneck Park 213
Blithewold Mansion 170
Brenton Point State Park 163
Green Animals 132
Patriot's Park 213
Seaman's Church Institute 168
Secret Garden Tours 170
Victorian Ladies, The 168
Wanton-Lyman-Hazard House 168

People
Beatrice Turner 134
Queen Elizabeth II 207

Performance and Theater
See also Live Music Venues
Festa Italiana 178
Irish Music Festival 177
Mrs. Astor's Beechwood 193
Newport Jazz Festival 179
Newport Blues Cafe 179
Red Parrot 180

Recreation and Fitness
See also Parks and Gardens
Adventure Water Sports 198
Aquidneck Park Tennis Courts 222
Bicycling Newport 229
Casino, The 220
Cliff Walk 154
Gooseberry Beach 143
Island Park Beach 143
Island Sports 218
Newport Yacht Charter 227
Newport Beaches 218
Newport Wheels 230
Newport Diving Center 161
Ocean State Scuba 161
Ocean State Adventures 198

SUBJECT INDEX

Paddle Sports, Newport 198
Sail Newport 208
Teddy's Beach 143
Ten Speed Spokes 230
Water Brothers Surf and Sport 218

Resources and Reference
Newport Historical Society 131,183 214

Restaurants
See also Ethnic Eating; Lunch and Light Meals; Vegetarian Havens
Asterix and Obelix 167
Cheeky Monkey, The 190
Dry Dock Seafood 212
Elizabeth's 220
Hisae's 179
Jamestown Oyster Bar and Grill 197
Las Petite Auberge 127
Le Bistro 145
Lucia 177
Music Hall Cafe 184
Nathaniel Porter Inn 196
Pizza Lucia 203
Puerini's 145, 226
Quito's 158
Red Parrot, The 162
Salvation Cafe 210
Scales & Shells 212
Sea Shai 179
Trattoria Sympatico 177
Via Via 203
West Deck, The 212
White Horse Tavern 137, 145

Sacred and Hallowed Places
Channing Memorial Church 153
Chapel by the Sea 148
Clifton Burial Ground 172
Common Ground Cemetery 171, 183, 214
Island Cemetery 172
Newport Congregational Church 153
Seaman's Church Institute 148
St. Columba Chapel 149
St. Spyridon's Greek Orthodox Church 173
Touro Synagogue 181, 199
Trinity Church 172, 207

Specialty and Craft Shops
See also Books and Literary Interests; Fashion, Clothing, and Accessories; Furniture and Home Design; Music Stores; Vintage and Antiques
Devonshire English Garden Shop 170
Gourmet Dog, The 199
High Flyers Flight Co. 186
Isle de France 229
J. H. Breakell, Silversmith 180
Runcible Spoon 185
Scrimshanders 211
Thames Glass 171

Sports
See also Recreation and Fitness
Cardines Field 141
Newport Polo Series 205
Tennis Hall of Fame 222

Statues and Public Art
See also Architecture and Buildings
Island Cemetery 172
Monkey Statue 190
Wave, The 215

Sweets
See also Coffee and Tea
Cappuccino's 146
Elizabeth's 220
Newport Chocolates 219
Newport Creamery 138

Tours and Trains
Block Island Ferry 223
Jamestown and Newport Ferry 223
Newport on Foot 223
Newport trolley 223
Newport on Foot 137
Rumrunner II 175
Secret Garden Tours 170
The Elms 140, 206

Trails
Cliff Walk 154

Vegetarian Havens
Lucia 177

Views
Cliff Walk 154
Marble House 225
Newport View Points 200

Vintage and Antiques

Aardvark, The 216
Army Navy Store 218
Euphoria! 180
Francis Malbone House 173
Norton's Oriental Gallery 178
Patriots' Shop 160
Samuel Whithorne House 193
The Griffon Shop 180

Waterfront

America's Cup 128
America's Cup Hall of Fame 129
Aquidneck Lobster 186
Block Island Ferry 223
Gooseberry Beach 143
Herreshoff Marine Museum 129
Island Park Beach 143
Island Sports 218
Jamestown and Newport Ferry 223
Long Wharf 213
Newport Yacht Charter 227
Ocean State Scuba 161
Paddle Sports In Newport 198
Rose Island Lighthouse 126
Rumrunner II 175
Sail Newport 208
Teddy's Beach 143
Water Brothers Surf and Sport 218
Yacht Restoration School 231

ALPHABETICAL INDEX

Providence

3 Steeple Street 31
Angelo's Civita Farnese 74
Annmary Brown Memorial 108
Arcade, The 99
AS220 51
Aspara 70
Bastille Day Restaurant Race 27
BEDLAM! 42
Beneficent Congregational Church 33
Benefit Street 21
Blackstone Valley Heritage Concerts 51
Blackstone River Valley National Heritage Corridor 111
Blackstone Valley Explorer 95
Blackstone River Theatre 49
Blackstone River State Park 80
Blackstone Boulevard 21
Bocce Club 33
Bowling Academy 105
Brickway On Wickenden 30
Brown University Jazz Band 50
Brown University Conservatory 65
Cable Car Cinema 35
Cafe Paragon 101
Cafe Yuni 71
Caffe Itri 65
Cape Verdian Independence Day 88
Castro, The 55
Center City Artisans 51
Chan's 34
Charles H. Smith Greenhouse 121
Chinese New Year 33
City Hall 90
Clown 39
Coffee Exchange 37
Copacetic Rudely Elegant Jewelry 69
Corliss-Bracket House 72
Cranston Country Club 56
Crescent Park Carousel 31
Dalrymple Boathouse 58
David Winton Bell Gallery 24
Diamond Hill Vineyards 118
Down Under Duckpin Bowling 103

Downcity 45
Dudek Bowling Alleys 103
East Bay Bike Path 80
Empire 49
Esta's Too 80
Ethnic Concepts 100
Fall Foliage Train Excursion 68
Federal Hill 64
Festival of Historic Houses 59
First Baptist Meeting House 25
Fleet Skating Center 63
Foxy Lady Club 68
Friends Market 87
Friends of the Blackstone 79
Gallery Night 23
Garden Grille 113
Goddard Memorial State Park 27
Goodie Basket, The 56
Governor Henry Lippett House 115
Greenwich Odeum 109
Hair-2-E-tan-ity 47
Hairspray 40
Helianthus 51
Hemenway's 75
Heritage Day 45
Iggy's Doughboys 44
India Point Park 83
International Holiday Sale 34
John Hay Library 90, 107
John Brown House 21
Johnson and Wales Culinary Museum 92
Jubilee Franco Americain 50
Kaplan's Bakery 36
L'Elizabeth 108
L'Osteria 65
L'Epicurio 64
La Gondola 115
Langston Hughes Center 28
Latin Christmas Carols 35
Leeds Theater 77
Lime Rock Preserve 121
Lincoln Woods State Park 111
Lisboa a Noite 88

Llama Farma, The 69
Lorraine Mill Fabrics 98
Loui's 100
Luminaria Candlelight Tour 61
Lupo's Heartbreak Hotel 76
Market House 108
Maximillian's Ice Cream 63
Mayor's Own Marinara Sauce 74
Met Cafe 77
Miko Exoticware 66
Monastery, The 75
Mounted Command Building 59
Museum of Natural History 42
Myopic Books 29
New Rivers 119
NewGate Theatre 77
Newport Jazz Festival 179
Ocean State Job Lot 82
Old Court, The 117
Olneyville New York System 119
Paddle Providence 79
Paddle Sports, Providence 79
Pakarang 108
Parking- Providence 83
Pasta Challenge 86
Pastiche 106
Pawtucket Red Sox 86
Pendragon 48
Perishable Theater 77
Prairie Diner 102
Prospect Park 88, 117
Providence Preservation Society 57
Providence Early Music Ensemble 50
Providence Zen Center 81
Providence Art Club 51
Providence Performing Arts Center 109
Providence Athenaeum 45
Providence Transport 112
Providence Biltmore 117
Public Restrooms, Providence 76
Rachel's Pastanova 86
Ran Zan 105
RI Labor and Ethnic Heritage Festival 67
RI School of Design Museum 112
RI Black Heritage Society 28
RI Watercolor Society 24
RI Historical Society Library 47
Roberto's Diner 82
Roger Williams Park Zoo 96
Roger Williams Park 80

Roger Williams Park Casino 118
Round Again Records 32
Rue de l'Espoir 30
Ryco Factory Outlet 98
Sabin Point Parrots 84
Samuel Slater Canal Boat 48
Sarah Doyle Gallery 51
Scialo Bros. Bakery 105
Seaplane Diner 102
Self Drive Foliage Tour 68
Serra d'Estrella 88
Shakespeare's Head 53
Slater Mill 67, 93
Slater Factory Fabrics 98
Slater Looff Carousel 31
Sliver Spring Golf Course 56
Spoons 102
Sportsman's Inn 58
St. Stephen's Church 57
State House 43
State House Inn 25
Stephen Hopkins House 53
Stuart Theater 77
Sunset Stables 59
Swan Point Cemetery 61
Taste of India 96
Tennis Rhode Island 37
Textile Warehouse 99
This & That Shop 24
Tilden-Thurber Co. 113
Tinsel Town and Patioland 35
Todd Marsilli Tennis Center 36
Triggs Memorial Golf Course 56
Trinity Repertory Company 93
Truman Beckwith House 53
Union Saint-Jean Baptiste D'Amerique 50
Valley Falls Park 94
Valley Park Cervezeria 87
Venda Ravioli 98
Veteran's Memorial Auditorium 77
Water Cruises 42
Water Ferry 40
WaterFire 28
Waterplace Park 21, 103
What Cheer! 94
Woods Gerry Mansion 72
Yarn Outlet, The 98
Ye Olde English Fish & Chips 48
Your Move Games 52

ALPHABETICAL INDEX

Newport

Aardvark, The 216
Accessible Newport 125
Adele Turner Inn 146, 220
Adventure Water Sports 198
Aiden's Pub 176
America's Cup Hall of Fame 129
America's Cup 128
Annex, The 132
Aquidneck Lobster 186
Aquidneck Park Tennis Courts 222
Aquidneck Park 213
Armchair Sailor, The 144
Army Navy Store 218
Artillery Company of Newport 134
Asterix and Obelix 167
Bay Voyage 184
Beatrice Turner 134
Beavertail State Park 144, 165
Belcourt Castle 136, 140
Bicycling Newport 229
Black History 213
Black Ships Festival 178
Blithewold Mansion 170
Block Island Ferry 223
Breakers Stable, The 155
Breakers, The 145, 148, 185, 205, 217
Brenton Point State Park 163
Brick Alley Pub 206
Butts Hill Fort 164
Cadeaux du Monde 162
Cappuccino's 146
Cardines Field 141
Casino, The 220
Channing Memorial Church 153
Chapel by the Sea 148
Chateau-sur-Mer 177, 225
Cheeky Monkey, The 156, 190
Chinese Tea House 219
Chowder Cook-off 151
Cliff Walk 154
Cliffside Inn 125, 135, 220
Clifton Burial Ground 172
Coanicut Island Sanctuary 143
Common Ground Cemetery 171, 183 214
Devonshire English Garden Shop 170
Dry Dock Seafood 212
Edward King House 166
Elizabeth's 220

Elm Tree Cottage 208
Elms Tea House, The 220
Elms, The 140, 206, 225, 228
Espresso Yourself Cafe 156
Euphoria! 180
Festa Italiana 178
Flo's Drive-in 167
Fort Hamilton 164
Fort Wetherill State Park 165, 224
Forty Steps 175
Francis Malbone House 173
Franklin Spa 145
Gooseberry Beach 143
Gourmet Dog, The 199
Green Galley, The 150
Green Animals 132, 195
Griffon Shop, The 180
Haffenreffer Museum of Anthropology 197
Haunted Newport 137
Herreshoff Marine Museum 129
High Flyers Flight Co. 186
Hisae's 179
Hunter House 156
Indigo Herbals 122
Irish Music Festival 177
Irish Heritage Month 176
Island Cemetery 172
Island Sports 218
Island Park Beach 143
Isle de France 229
Ivy Lodge 192
J. H. Breakell, Silversmith 180
Jamestown Oyster Bar and Grill 197
Jamestown and Newport Ferry 223
Jamestown Wind Mill 230
Jane Pickens Theater 192
Jonnycakes 181
Joshua & Co. 148
King Phillip's Seat 198
Kingscote 187
Las Petite Auberge 127
Le Bistro 145
Lilly's of the Alley 160
Long Wharf 213
Lucia 177
Marble House 225, 229
Market, The 201
May Breakfast 181

Melville Pond Campground 147
Monkey Statue 190
Movies Filmed in Newport 191
Mrs. Astor's Beechwood 193
Mudville's Pub 141
Museum of Newport History 163, 184
Music Hall Cafe 184
Nathaniel Porter Inn 196
Naval War College 210
Newport Diving Center 161
Newport Chocolates 219
Newport Congregational Church 153
Newport Blues Cafe 179
Newport Attractions for Kids 183
Newport Beaches 218
Newport Deals 159
Newport Art Museum 144
Newport Flower Show 203
Newport Wheels 230
Newport Equestrian Center 155
Newport Trees 225
Newport transportation 223
Newport Historical Society 131, 183, 214
Newport on Foot 137, 223
Newport Polo Series 205
Newport Yacht Charter 227
Newport Playgrounds 204
Newport View Points 200
Newport Aquarium 161
Newport Creamery 138
Newport Jazz Venues 180
Newport Kite Festival 186
Nikolas Pizza 173
Norman Bird Sanctuary 143
Norton's Oriental Gallery 178
Ocean State Scuba 161
Ocean State Adventures 198
Ochre Court 166
Old Stone Mill 189
Paddle Sports, Newport 198
Patriot's Park 213
Patriots' Shop 160
Petite Auberge 137
Pineapple Grill, The 196
Pizza Lucia 203
Point, The 156
Prescott Farm 230
Preservation Society of Newport County 165
Prohibition 175
Public Restrooms, Newport 195

Puerini's 145, 226
Purgatory Chasm 149
Queen Elizbeth II 207
Quito's 158
Red Parrot, The 162, 180
Redwood Library 133
Rose Island Lighthouse 126, 138
Rose Island 144
Rosecliff 147
Rough Point 188
Rumrunner II 175
Runcible Spoon 185
Sachuest National Wildlife Refuge 143
Sail Newport 208
Salvation Cafe 210, 222
Samuel Whithorne House 193
Scales & Shells 212
Scribe's Perch Bookstore, The 144
Scrimshanders 211
Sea Shai 179
Seaman's Church Institute 125, 148, 168
Secret Garden Tours 170
Slice of Heaven 201
St. Patrick's Day Parade 176
St. Columba Chapel 149
St. Spyridon's Greek Orthodox Church 173
Swiss Village 227
Sydney L. Wright Museum 195
Tatters 151
Tea & Herb Essence 133
Teddy's Beach 143
Ten Speed Spokes 230
Tennis Hall of Fame 222
Thames Glass 171
Touro Synagogue 181, 199
Trattoria Sympatico 177
Trinity Church 172, 207, 214
Tropical Fish 161
Vanderbilt Hall 220
Via Via 203
Victorian Ladies, The 168
Wanton-Lyman-Hazard House 168
Water Brothers Surf and Sport 218
Wave, The 215
Weekend of Coaching 155
West Deck, The 212
White Horse Tavern 137, 145
White Lady 128
Yacht Restoration School 231